CONFLICT

is for the

BIRDS

UNDERSTANDING YOUR CONFLICT MANAGEMENT STYLE

by Gayle Wiebe Oudeh & Nabil Oudeh

Dedicated to

Ameena and Nadeem

In loving memory

Marge, Omar,
and Mahmood

ACKNOWLEDGEMENTS

We've been avid bird-watchers for years. As conflict resolution practitioners we have experienced the destructive and constructive dynamics of conflict management styles. In workshops, conferences and other public forums, we have shared our observations on how conflict management styles interact, clash, and assist in resolving conflicts. Every time we talked about *the birds* we found people willing to share their own stories. Every conversation, story, and illustration added to the richness of our understanding of how people behave in conflict situations and why we adopt those behaviors.

It became clear to us that using the metaphor of the birds was helpful when talking about conflict management behaviors. It made a difficult and often intimidating subject much more accessible and sometimes even entertaining. While we claim the birds as our own invention we gratefully acknowledge the work of Robert Blake and Jane Mouton who wrote *The Managerial Grid* in the early 1960s. Their work on leadership styles led them to develop a grid not unlike the one described in this book. In their studies, Blake and Mouton looked at various aspects of leadership including approaches to managing conflict. Today their initial work on conflict management theory is widely accepted and used by conflict resolution practitioners, theoreticians and academics around the world. Blake and Mouton's work served as the foundation for our own research and understanding of how people behave in conflict situations.

In our practice we recognized the need for individuals to assess their own conflict management styles and developed the questionnaire that is included in this book. The version you see here is one that has been refined, tweaked, and tested over a seven-year period. We want to thank all our workshop participants who completed the questionnaire and generously gave us feedback on its accessibility and usefulness. Many of our colleagues also assisted us in developing the questionnaire by sharing their knowledge with us. We would be remiss, however, if we did not single out one colleague. Gerri Cooper's linguistic sensitivities and expertise as well as her organizational skills were instrumental in developing the format, structure, and final version of the statements found in the questionnaire. Thank you, Gerri.

As we used this questionnaire in training sessions, workshops, and seminars people kept asking us when we were going to write a book on the birds. The encouragement we received was overwhelming, humbling, and at times intimidating. We had spoken about the birds so often but could we put our many thoughts, observations, and anecdotes into writing? And could we do it while maintaining our consulting practice and an active family life?

The simple answer, of course, is no. At least not without a great deal of help. We consider ourselves fortunate to have received the support and assistance we needed to make this book a reality.

A huge thank you goes to our CCR International family. By taking on some of our workload you gave us the time and space we needed to write. Your enthusiasm and encouraging words were instrumental in continuing our pursuit of this dream. Your helpful comments, suggestions, and insights are a part of what is written here.

Many of the examples and stories that are interwoven throughout this book come from the very real stories shared with us by workshop participants, colleagues, family, and friends. We thank all of those who shared their personal lives with us in this way. Some of the stories are also taken from our own practice. Here we have altered details and developed composite stories – while the individuals described in our stories are not identifiable, the themes and the experiences are very real.

Our words have been greatly enhanced by the outstanding artwork of Rodrigo Riedel. His artistry and immediate understanding of what we were looking for made him a pleasure to work with. His contribution to this book has meant a great deal to us. Thank you, Rodrigo.

Thank you also to Collin Young who did an outstanding job of listening to our ramblings and then designing a beautiful book cover.

Our extended families were helpful beyond measure by providing childcare, feeding us, and sometimes even taking over the household – all to allow us the opportunity to get that next chapter written. Thank you isn't a big enough word to let you know how much we appreciated your love and support through this whole process.

Certain family members also gave of their expertise, which we found invaluable. Curt, your knowledge of the world of printers and publishers made you a constant resource to us. Candice, your attention to detail and your insightful comments made the editing process creative and pain-free. Eugene, your patience and ability to make this look like the book we wanted it to be resulted in a lot of laughter and some very special memories. Thank you!

The people most affected by this project were our two children, Ameena and Nadeem. Many times they would ask us, "are you *still* writing those bird stories?" and yet they were endlessly patient with us and wonderfully excited for us. Throughout this process they reminded us about what is really important in life. Thank you for being the very special people that you are.

TABLE OF CONTENTS

INTRODUCTION

Conflict is for the birds! It's a real pain in the neck! How can anything good come out of conflict? These are comments and questions that we have heard many, many times in over twenty years of practice in the conflict resolution field.

It is rare to come across someone whose first thought about a conflict is its positive potential. We're so sure that conflict is going to be painful and nasty that we don't see the possibility of anything else. We're so overwhelmed by the negative possibilities of conflict that we can't see how anything good can come out of it.

For most of us, our negative attitudes are long-standing, deep-seated, and very difficult to change. When we see conflict as destructive, we expect an unpleasant experience every time we have a conflict. Our response to the conflict and our behavior in the conflict directly correlates with our attitudes and expectations. Because we are expecting the worst, our behaviors reflect this. And guess what? It becomes a self-fulfilling prophecy. Because we expect it to be negative we behave as if it will be negative and because we behave as if it will be negative, it usually is!

But conflict also has the potential to be positive. We can unleash the positive potential in conflict situations by responding to the conflict in a healthy and appropriate way. This isn't easy for us to do. We're often stuck in certain patterns of behavior when it comes to conflict. "That's how I am - that's how I react," we say. But we do have choices. We can choose how we will respond to conflict.

The first step is exploring and understanding our behavior in conflict situations. The pattern in how we handle conflict is called our conflict management style. When we recognize our conflict management style we can learn when this style works for us and when it does more harm than good.

There are five distinct conflict management styles. Each of these styles has their unique strengths and their unique challenges. In order to more clearly understand these five conflict management styles we have chosen to identify these styles as the Woodpecker, the Parakeet, the Ostrich, the Owl, and the Hummingbird. We have found that each conflict management style has some interesting parallels to the characteristics of these five birds.

Are you a Woodpecker when dealing with conflict, hammering at issues? A Hummingbird who shifts positions easily? Are you an Owl, needing all the facts? Or a Parakeet, always aiming to please and chirping pleasantries? Perhaps you're an Ostrich, who would rather flee than fight?

In this book you will have an opportunity to explore your behaviors in conflict situations and identify your conflict management style. Included is a questionnaire that will help you determine if your conflict management style has the characteristics of a woodpecker, parakeet, owl, ostrich or hummingbird. Following the questionnaire are individual chapters on each of the five conflict management styles. These chapters take an in-depth look at each style – the characteristics and tactics of the style as well as when it is useful and when it's not. You will also find out what happens when you use this conflict management style too often and how to avoid using it inappropriately. Finally, each chapter gives you some useful tips on how to deal with others who use this particular conflict management style.

As you determine your conflict management style you will gain a greater understanding of the strengths and challenges that are inherent in each style. You will learn what happens when the feathers fly and your conflict management style comes head to head with someone else's conflict management style. And you will learn how to determine the most appropriate way to deal with conflict situations in the future.

You can experience the positive potential of conflict because conflict really is for the birds – Woodpeckers, Parakeets, Owls, Ostriches and Hummingbirds, that is!

1

RUFFLED FEATHERS
Understanding Our Attitudes Toward Conflict

How Conflict Starts

Our first house was an old character home that needed continual maintenance. Knowing that it is important to learn from our mistakes, we decided when it was time to move to a new city, that character homes were not for us. Since we're not handy fixer-upper types we bought a 40-year-old house instead of a 90-year-old house. When we moved into our new home, we noticed a bubble in the paint of the ceiling of the main floor bathroom. It was a small bubble, no more than three inches in diameter. We looked at it and thought, " Oh, this is not a big deal. It's just an air bubble. We'll have to scrape that down and repaint." But since it wasn't an emergency, it didn't get done. A year passed and one day our daughter asked, "Daddy, what is that?" pointing at the ceiling of the bathroom. It did seem that the air bubble in the paint had increased in size somewhat but we assured our daughter that it was not a big problem and we just needed to repaint the bathroom. Three years later, when we decided to move across the country and needed to put our house on the market, we took another look at that air bubble. It really had increased in size. We realized that potential buyers might be concerned about this air bubble. We decided to repaint. We began by sanding down the air bubble. It seemed that there were sections of the ceiling plaster that were no longer solid so we started poking around the edges of the air bubble. Within minutes, a section of plaster about half the size of the bathroom ceiling came tumbling down. Undaunted, we patched up the hole and repainted. Within a week the air bubble was back, bigger than ever. The quick patch up job hadn't worked. You can probably guess what happened next. It was clear that we needed professional help. A few thousand dollars later, we had a totally renovated bathroom.

Like that air bubble, conflict often starts out as something that doesn't appear overly significant on the surface. And so we ignore it. We expect it to go away or, at the very least, not to affect us in any momentous way. We really don't want to have to deal with it. Time passes. The conflict is still there, in the back of our minds. And then, someone says something or does something and the conflict is back, in full force. In fact, it has probably increased in intensity because it's been brewing for so long.

We can have the opposite response to conflict as well. We don't ignore it – we jump in with both feet! It can flare out of control almost instantaneously. This happens when our reaction to the conflict is out of proportion with the conflict itself. We overreact.

A friend of ours who is a newspaper reporter told us of a story he had covered for his local paper that is an example of this type of overreaction. In his community there was an incident involving a car and a pick up truck. Police were alerted to a situation where the car was dangerously chasing the pick up truck. When the police got involved in the pursuit, the pick up truck pulled over but the car continued to evade the police. The chase persisted with several police cars getting involved. The car raced up and down residential streets, driving over lawns and hitting several parked cars, still managing to outrun the police. Eventually the car stopped and the driver ran out of the car and into the nearest house. Police were not sure if the house was occupied or if it was the driver's home. Police surrounded the house and sent in the police dogs first to try to get the driver to come out. Eventually the driver was captured and arrested.

What is interesting about this situation is how it started. The driver of the car had accidentally cut off the driver of the pick up truck on the freeway. The driver of the truck, angry about being cut off, had pulled up beside the car at a stoplight, got out of his truck, and broke the passenger side window of the car with a wrench. The driver of the car then began chasing the truck and the police got involved. The end result was thousands of dollars worth of damage and two arrested drivers. All because one vehicle had pulled in too closely in front of another vehicle!

Images Of Conflict

When we run conflict resolution skills workshops, we frequently ask participants to describe a thought or image that comes to mind when they think of conflict. One participant quickly explained that, to her, conflict was like a toothache. It often begins as a nagging, almost subtle, pain. It's always there. Although we can ignore the pain for a time it doesn't go away. And, little by little, day-by-day, the pain intensifies. Before long there's no getting around it, something has to be done. All the painkillers in the world won't take care of that toothache. A trip to the dentist is required. The anticipation of going to the dentist and the potential needles, drills and scrapers is frightening. Not to mention the bill we'll have to pay at the end of it all! So we think maybe we can live with the toothache after all. We put off the visit for a little while longer. Finally the pain becomes so unbearable that a trip to the dentist cannot be avoided. The actual dental procedure may not be as bad as we had envisioned but it's no walk in the park either. And, after it's all over, we're numb!

Conflict can be like a toothache but it can also be like a tornado. Sometimes conflict hits us with almost no warning. Everything seemed so calm and suddenly, within minutes, there is an intensity of emotions that we simply weren't expecting. This type of conflict often moves in and out very quickly. And no one can really predict what direction it will take. Sometimes these conflicts barely touch down. Others are so intense that the destruction left in its wake is devastating.

The fact is life does not exist without conflict. We're individuals with individual wants, needs and expectations. Sooner or later our individuality rubs up against someone else's individuality and the result is CONFLICT!

What Is Conflict?

Conflict is differing or opposing needs, wants or expectations. It happens when you're watching the news and the kids want to watch their favorite cartoons. Or your list of things to do is beckoning and your colleague wants to compare notes about what you did this weekend. It happens when you've been at home all day with the children and need some adult interaction but your spouse wants time to unwind and doesn't feel like talking. Or when you ordered a tossed salad with your sandwich and your order arrives with Caesar salad instead. It also happens when you've brought the woman you plan to marry home to mom and dad and they tell you they don't think she's right for you. Conflicts come in all shapes and sizes but one thing is certain – we all experience them.

Conflict occurs in every type of relationship. It occurs whenever our assumptions or expectations don't match with someone else's assumptions or expectations – they *pinch*. So, when our spouse makes plans for a golf game with his buddies on Saturday and we assumed that he was going to help with a weekend painting project, this *pinch* of our assumptions causes conflict. When we have completed a task at work and expect the boss to praise our efforts and all we get is an impersonal nod, our expectations get another *pinch* and we've got conflict.

Big or small, these pinches happen all the time. And when they occur, our stress and anxiety increases and we are often unable or unwilling to effectively communicate with the other party. Left unchecked, the conflict escalates. Our emotions are engaged. So the next time our spouse seems to put personal plans before home maintenance or our boss seems to take us for granted it's not just a *pinch* anymore! The situation has become painful and we can't stand it. The conflict must be dealt with. And like that trip to the dentist or like the tornado, once the conflict is at this stage, dealing with it is rarely pleasant. It's often upsetting, frequently messy, and sometimes enormously destructive.

Attitudes Toward Conflict

Our reluctance to deal with a conflict at that initial *pinch* point is due to our attitudes toward conflict. Most of us have very negative attitudes about conflict. The anticipation of a confrontation starts a fluttering in our stomachs. An angry exchange leaves our hearts pounding. Remember that workshop participant who said that to her conflict was like a toothache? Try asking people about their images of conflict. You will hear things like "fire", "thunderstorm", "the flu", "a migraine", "rotten fruit", "a battle ground" and on and on. For most of us, conflict is a bad word. It conjures up mental images of destruction and chaos. It makes us feel out of control. It seems unpredictable. Our attitude toward conflict is overwhelmingly negative. And, because our attitude toward conflict is negative, our expectation is that dealing with a conflict situation will be a negative experience.

When aspiring teachers are training in University, one of their greatest concerns is classroom discipline. They want to know the how's, when's, and what's of maintaining order in the classroom. A University professor, recognizing the significance of this issue to his students, decided to present a special lecture on discipline in the classroom. The lecture was very well attended. But what he said was that there are no magic how's, when's and what's of discipline. The key to classroom discipline is the teacher's expectations. He said, "If you expect your students to misbehave, you can be guaranteed that they will. If you expect them to behave, their behavior may not be perfect, but it will be better." The same can be said of people in conflict. If you expect the results of confronting a conflict to be negative, you can be guaranteed that they will be negative. If you expect the results to be positive, they may not be perfect, but they will be better.

Our attitudes and expectations affect our behavior. Because we expect a conflict to be a negative experience, we react in ways that allow the conflict situation to escalate. In responding this way, any positive potential in the conflict gets lost. And our negative attitudes are reinforced. We say to ourselves, "See, I knew trying to deal with this conflict would end badly. I don't ever want to go through something like that again. Conflict is destructive." We get caught in a negative cycle that is very difficult to break out of. It looks something like this:

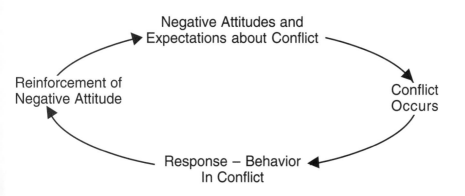

This doesn't have to be a negative cycle. It can be positive. The key, of course, is our attitudes and expectations. If we have positive attitudes and expectations, our behavior in conflict situations changes and the results are more positive. If our results are more positive, our positive attitudes and expectations are reinforced.

All we have to do is think more positively about conflict. Do a little reframing. Rather than see conflict as negative, see it as an opportunity for better communication, greater clarity and enhanced relationships. "Yeah right!" you're probably thinking right now. "If only it were that easy!" For most of us, our negative attitudes about conflict have been reinforced by years and years of experience. It's not so easy to just decide one day to have a more positive attitude.

But there is one part of that negative cycle that we do have some control over. We do have control over our *response* to conflict. We know that conflict is going to happen – it is inevitable. We can't control that. But we have choices to make in our response to conflict. If we start to respond to conflict in a positive and appropriate way, we will have more constructive experiences with conflict. This, in turn, will influence our attitudes and expectations.

We can break that negative cycle. We need to start by examining our response to conflict – how we behave in conflict situations. Once we recognize our own behaviors and their impact on the outcome of any conflict situation, we can start to make the appropriate changes.

Responses To Conflict

Think about how you respond to conflict. Do you tend to be confrontational or more appeasing? Do you avoid conflict as long as you possibly can or would you rather negotiate a quick settlement? Or do you prefer to delve into all aspects of the situation and thoroughly examine every option?

You have a preferred conflict management style. Your conflict management style is likely not something you've intentionally adopted. In fact, many of us are dissatisfied with how we respond to conflict. And yet, when we find ourselves in conflict situations, we react the same way time and time again. Why? Because our conflict management style is something that has been learned and reinforced over time by our experiences.

Remember when you were a kid and you didn't like a decision or a rule set by your parents? You said to yourself "When I'm an adult or a parent, I'll never be like that, or do that, or treat my kids that way." And then, as an adult, you find yourself in a situation where you're doing or saying exactly what you vowed you'd never do or say. And suddenly you realize "Oh no, I've turned into my parents. How did that happen?" It happened because those messages from our parents, right or wrong, good or bad, are deeply embedded in our psyche. Even when we say to ourselves that we don't want to be that way, those messages don't automatically disappear. And, in vulnerable moments, when we are not consciously thinking about what to do or say in a particular situation, those old messages can pop out and suddenly, there it is – our parents words but in our own voice!

The way we respond to conflict is much the same. Unless we are very consciously considering our response, we tend to fall back on those subconscious behaviors that we learned long ago. A friend told us about her mother's constant reference to the old adage *If you can't say something nice, don't say anything at all.*

"My mother used that cliché almost every day. It was drummed into us. And we learned to smile and be pleasant no matter what the circumstance. So we never talked about conflict. It was not acceptable to get into an argument. Even now, with a family of my own, I hear my mother's voice whenever I get annoyed with someone. And my immediate reaction is to avoid any type of confrontation with the other person."

For some of us, our conflict management style has been learned in the workplace. One gentleman told us of his long career in a manufacturing plant. "I started working there right out of high school. And it was clear almost immediately that it was a dog-eat-dog environment. It was a union shop and we had to fight for everything. Being loud and stubborn was the only way to get anywhere. Anything less was considered weak and if you were weak you wouldn't survive. I learned how to speak up and refuse to back down. Now I never back away from a fight. And if I see the other party hesitating in any way, I know I've won."

The way we behave in conflict situations becomes so ingrained in us that it seems instinctive. Wherever or however we've learned to respond to conflict, our conflict management style shows up whenever we are not deliberately or intentionally choosing how to behave. And that's probably most of the time.

Conflict is one of those vulnerable moments. We often don't see it coming or are surprised by its level of intensity. We may know that our friend is upset but have no idea why the friend confronts us with "You jerk! How dare you say that I'm unreliable! You're the one who's unreliable! Remember when you said you were going to meet me at eight last week? It was almost nine before you showed up! But now when I'm a few minutes late I'm unreliable?" Because we didn't see this conflict coming, our reaction is on automatic pilot. Our instinctive conflict management style comes into play. We may attempt to confront our friend just as we have been confronted. Or we may reason with our friend, either pointing out the insignificance of the argument, or simply agreeing that we probably were jerks in this instance. We may end up talking at length about the many times either or both of us has been disappointed in the other. Or we may try to disengage from the conflict all together. Depending on the situation and the people involved, some of these styles will be more effective than others.

We can get trapped in patterns of behavior that are ineffective because our conflict management style is a reflex reaction. We may find that when we get involved in a conflict it frequently gets out of control and we don't know why. Or the solution to a situation may seem simple enough to us but the other party just refuses to see reason. Or our resentment remains long after the actual confrontation and, to make matters worse, the other party seems to have forgotten the incident completely! All of these experiences reinforce our attitude that conflict is a distressing and harmful experience.

The conflict we experience in our lives does not have to be destructive. Another workshop participant once told us that, to her, conflict was like a potato. A potato seems inoffensive. Potatoes are a staple – most of us have potatoes in our kitchens. But if that potato sits around for too long and we don't do anything with it, it will rot. If you've ever smelled a rotting potato you know how unpleasant it is. Rotting potatoes are a mess – not only do they smell bad, they also stain the container they're stored in. So, even once you throw out the rotten potato, you're stuck with a stain and a lingering odor.

But a potato also has amazing potential if you use it before it goes bad. Potatoes can be cooked in numerous ways resulting in a wide array of delicious and satisfying dishes. You can even cut up a potato, plant it, and grow more potato plants that can feed you for weeks to come.

Conflict is like a potato. Conflict can be a horrible experience but it doesn't have to be. We can make conflict work positively for us. Understanding our conflict management styles and breaking free from those ineffective patterns is the key. We can control our reactions to conflict rather than allowing knee-jerk reactions to control us. We can learn to respond to conflict in a healthy and effective way. By making a clear and deliberate choice about how we respond to conflict we can explore the positive potential of conflict. We can discover the productivity and creativity that is the result of well-managed conflict.

2

WHEN THE FEATHERS FLY
Determining Your Conflict Management Style

Conflict Behavior Patterns

"Whenever my husband and I argue," a neighbor told us, "it seems to play out the same way. I say something in the heat of the moment. I'm not really thinking. I'm just ready to say almost anything so that we can get back on track and not have to deal with the conflict any longer. But my husband picks up on some little aspect of what I've said and will then suggest that we *take a moment to analyze this*. He'll want to discuss why I said what I said and what I *really* meant by it. If he had his way we'd spend the next ten hours having a real heart-to-heart. Sometimes it drives me crazy. So instead of explaining what I meant because, frankly, it was not some great self-disclosing declaration on my part, I'll try to suggest a compromise. Every time he asks why I've made a particular suggestion, rather than explain and rationalize, I'll come up with another option. Eventually one of us will wear the other one out. Either he'll agree to a solution I've suggested and that's the end of it or we end up hashing through the whole thing for hours on end. It doesn't seem to matter what the conflict is about. The way we react to any disagreement follows the same pattern over and over again."

If you think about your own experiences with conflict, you can probably start to recognize some of the patterns in your own behavior. The following questionnaire is intended to look at those patterns and help you determine your dominant conflict management style.

There are one hundred items in this questionnaire. The first fifty items ask you to rate a statement on a scale of "1 to 5" where "1" is least like you and "5" is most like you. Each statement begins with "When I am in a conflict situation, I ... " and concludes with a description of an attitude or behavior. Consider how well this statement describes you in a general way in *most* conflict situations. Don't think only of particularly disastrous confrontations; consider day-to-day conflicts with family, friends and colleagues as well. If the statement describes your behavior or attitude most of the time (rarely will it describe you all of the time), rate it at a "5." If it describes how you respond to conflict a lot of the time rate it at a "4." Give it a "3" if the statement describes you some of the time, a "2" if it describes your attitude or behavior occasionally. You should rate the statement a "1" if it is an attitude or behavior that almost never describes you. Put your rating of each statement in the appropriate shaded box.

The last fifty items are word pairs. Consider the two words presented and choose the word that most accurately describes your attitude or behavior in conflict situations. This portion of the questionnaire is forced-choice. Choose the word that describes you best. In some cases you may feel that both words describe you, in other cases you may feel that neither word describes you. You must choose only one word. It should be the word that describes you most of the time or the one that describes you more than the other.

You may find that as you consider the statements and word pairs, your responses would be significantly different depending on whom you are in conflict with. For example, you may feel that you respond very differently to conflicts with your colleagues in the workplace than you do to conflicts with your spouse. If this is the case, consider where you experience conflict most frequently. If you rarely have conflicts with your colleagues but frequently experience conflicts with your spouse, answer the questions based on your conflict behaviors with your spouse.

As with most questionnaires of this nature, it is preferable that you don't think too long and hard about your response to each statement or word pair. Your immediate, instinctual response is usually the best response. If you have particular difficulty in responding to a statement or word pair, skip over that one for the moment and come back to it after you have completed the rest of the questionnaire. In order for the questionnaire to be accurate it is important that you respond to all statements and all word pairs. Be as objective and realistic as possible. Rate the statements and choose words based on what you actually do, not what you would like to do!

Remember that there are no answers that are better or worse, right or wrong. As you will discover, there are appropriate uses for all conflict management styles. There are also unique challenges that come with each conflict management style. This questionnaire will highlight your preferences or patterns as you respond to conflict. Once you have determined your conflict management style you can gain a greater understanding of your unique strengths and challenges when dealing with conflict.

Conflict Management Styles Questionnaire

Part A

Place the numerical answer (numbers between 1 and 5) for each question in the gray shaded section. At the bottom of each page add the numbers in each column and enter the totals in the bottom row. Transfer the totals to the corresponding columns on the next page.

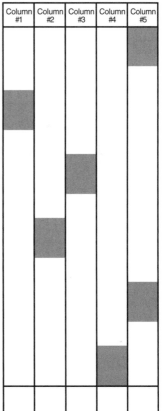

	Column #1	Column #2	Column #3	Column #4	Column #5
When I am in a conflict situation, I do not let concerns about the relationship between the other and myself stop me from pursuing my goals.					▨
When I am in a conflict situation, I make sure that we each understand the other's relevant issues.	▨				
When I am in a conflict situation, I try to meet both our needs.			▨		
When I am in a conflict situation, I avoid discussing the matter with the other person.		▨			
When I am in a conflict situation, I am not afraid to pursue the situation aggressively.					▨
When I am in a conflict situation, I try to "keep the peace" by putting aside my needs.				▨	
TOTALS					

TOTALS
(From previous page)

When I am in a conflict situation, I try to integrate our solutions.

When I am in a conflict situation, I prefer to meet in the middle.

When I am in a conflict situation, I prefer to take an indirect approach to resolution.

When I am in a conflict situation, I usually look for a quick resolution.

When I am in a conflict situation, I find it difficult to defend my personal interests.

When I am in a conflict situation, I am not prepared to compromise when I am right.

When I am in a conflict situation, I find that the potential outcome of confronting the other person is not worth the energy or effort.

When I am in a conflict situation, I prefer to discuss the matter until we are both completely satisfied.

When I am in a conflict situation, I try to get some of what I want rather than everything I want.

When I am in a conflict situation, I try to concentrate on our areas of agreement.

TOTALS (include totals from top of page)

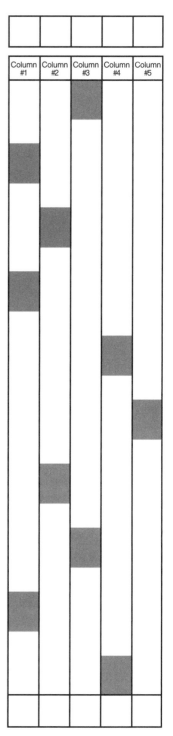

TOTALS
(From previous page)

	Column #1	Column #2	Column #3	Column #4	Column #5
(Totals from previous page)					
When I am in a conflict situation, I prefer to joke or charm my way out of the situation.		▨			
When I am in a conflict situation, I want to win.					▨
When I am in a conflict situation, I look for a solution where everyone is required to yield to the group.			▨		
When I am in a conflict situation, I say what the other person wants to hear in order to resolve the conflict.				▨	
When I am in a conflict situation, I pull back to minimize tension.		▨			
When I am in a conflict situation, I want to keep on working until we come to my desired resolution.					▨
When I am in a conflict situation, I do not allow time constraints to limit my attempts at resolution.			▨		
When I am in a conflict situation, I am immediately prepared to negotiate.	▨				
When I am in a conflict situation, I will concede to please the other person.				▨	
When I am in a conflict situation, I believe that listening to negative feedback is a waste of time.					▨
TOTALS (include totals from top of page)					

TOTALS
(From previous page)

	Column #1	Column #2	Column #3	Column #4	Column #5

When I am in a conflict situation, I work for a mutually agreeable solution based on give and take.

When I am in a conflict situation, I try to work creatively with the other person to find new options.

When I am in a conflict situation, I believe that our disagreements are not worth worrying about.

When I am in a conflict situation, I am not afraid to defend the unpopular view.

When I am in a conflict situation, I don't hesitate to acknowledge when I am wrong.

When I am in a conflict situation, I treat every issue as having equal importance.

When I am in a conflict situation, I try to meet the other person half way.

When I am in a conflict situation, I prefer to wait for the situation to resolve itself rather than taking action.

When I am in a conflict situation, I tend to evaluate the situation, and look for solutions somewhere in the middle.

When I am in a conflict situation, I give more attention to the other person's feelings than to my own issues.

TOTALS (include totals from top of page)

TOTALS
(From previous page)

	Column #1	Column #2	Column #3	Column #4	Column #5
When I am in a conflict situation, I am not afraid to say the difficult things.					■
When I am in a conflict situation, I will withdraw if the situation becomes heated.		■			
When I am in a conflict situation, I prefer to work together on a solution.			■		
When I am in a conflict situation, I want to identify the other person's issues so that we can make a deal.	■				
When I am in a conflict situation, my priority is protecting the relationship, rather than defending the rules.				■	
When I am in a conflict situation, I try to keep a safe distance from those with whom I disagree.		■			
When I am in a conflict situation, my primary concerns are my values and principles.					■
When I am in a conflict situation, I work for a resolution that is absolutely fair to both parties.			■		
When I am in a conflict situation, I make sure that the problem doesn't interfere with our relationship.				■	
When I am in a conflict situation, I avoid taking controversial positions.		■			

TOTALS (include totals from top of page)

TOTALS
(From previous page)

When I am in a conflict situation, I concentrate on conveying the logic and benefits of my position.

When I am in a conflict situation, I try to work with the other person to maximize success for each.

When I am in a conflict situation, I will shift my objectives in order to come to a quick resolution.

When I am in a conflict situation, I try to smooth things out.

PART A TOTALS

	Column #1	Column #2	Column #3	Column #4	Column #5

PART B

Forward part A totals to the appropriate row.

For each word pair select the word that most accurately reflects your attitude or behaviour in conflict situations. Put an "x" in the gray shaded area beside your word choice. At the bottom of each page add the number of "x's" in each column. Add these numbers to your Part A totals and enter your new totals in the bottom row. Transfer the totals to the corresponding columns on the next page.

	Column #1	Column #2	Column #3	Column #4	Column #5
PART A TOTALS					

	Column #1	Column #2	Column #3	Column #4	Column #5
Collaborate Come to terms					
Disengage Conform					
TOTALS (include totals from top of page)					

TOTALS
(From previous page)

	Column #1	Column #2	Column #3	Column #4	Column #5
I Us					
Contest Negotiate					
Plan Refrain					
Compromise Surrender					
You Us					
Strive Dodge					
Insist Settle					
Attack Integrate					
Meet halfway Assert					
Give Contend					
Accompany Surrender					
They We					

TOTALS (include totals from top of page)

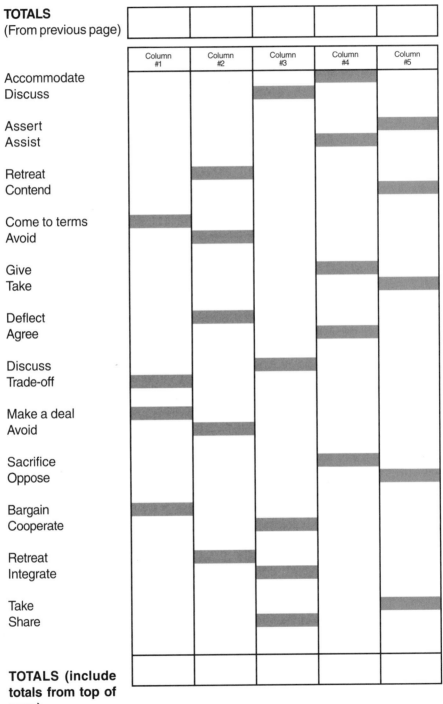

TOTALS
(From previous page)

	Column #1	Column #2	Column #3	Column #4	Column #5
Accommodate				▓	
Discuss			▓		
Assert					▓
Assist				▓	
Retreat		▓			
Contend					▓
Come to terms	▓				
Avoid		▓			
Give				▓	
Take					▓
Deflect		▓			
Agree				▓	
Discuss			▓		
Trade-off	▓				
Make a deal	▓				
Avoid		▓			
Sacrifice				▓	
Oppose					▓
Bargain	▓				
Cooperate			▓		
Retreat		▓			
Integrate			▓		
Take					▓
Share			▓		

TOTALS (include totals from top of page)

	Column #1	Column #2	Column #3	Column #4	Column #5
TOTALS (From previous page)					
Cooperate			▨		
Give and Take	▨				
You				▨	
I					▨
Disengage		▨			
Surrender				▨	
Come to Terms	▨				
Concede				▨	
Disengage		▨			
Integrate			▨		
You				▨	
They		▨			
Evade		▨			
Give and Take	▨				
Attack					▨
Deflect		▨			
Discuss			▨		
Agree				▨	
Disengage		▨			
Oppose					▨
Compromise	▨				
Contest					▨
Negotiate	▨				
Give				▨	
TOTALS (include totals from top of page)					

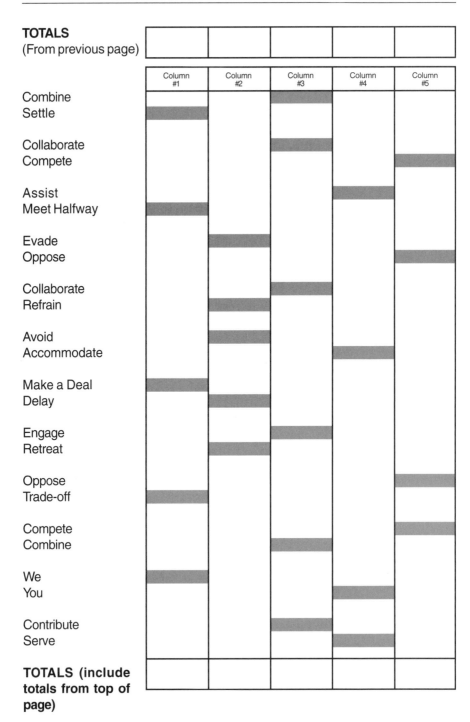

TOTALS
(From previous page)

	Column #1	Column #2	Column #3	Column #4	Column #5
Combine			▓		
Settle	▓				
Collaborate			▓		
Compete					▓
Assist				▓	
Meet Halfway	▓				
Evade		▓			
Oppose					▓
Collaborate			▓		
Refrain		▓			
Avoid		▓			
Accommodate				▓	
Make a Deal	▓				
Delay		▓			
Engage			▓		
Retreat		▓			
Oppose					▓
Trade-off	▓				
Compete					▓
Combine			▓		
We	▓				
You				▓	
Contribute			▓		
Serve				▓	

TOTALS (include totals from top of page)

The Five Conflict Management Styles

The five different conflict management styles can best be understood if you consider them on a grid. The grid has two axes. One axis deals with your concern for satisfying your own needs (focus on self). The other axis considers your desire to resolve the conflict to the satisfaction of the other party (focus on other). Insert your scores into the following grid. Your highest score is your dominant conflict management style.

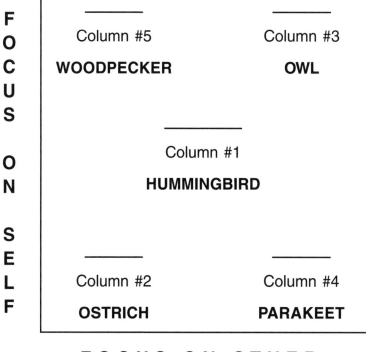

Look at your highest score. This is the conflict management style that you use most often. It has its advantages as well as its drawbacks but, for better or worse, it is the conflict management style that you have adopted.

You are a Woodpecker if your concern is largely for resolving conflict your way and you have very little concern for resolving the conflict to the satisfaction of the other party. The Woodpecker is high on the *focus on self* axis but low on the *focus on other* axis. Woodpeckers are often said to be very competitive because they see every conflict as a challenge that they are determined to win. "Do it my way" is the Woodpecker's attitude in conflict situations.

You are a Parakeet if your concern is mostly for the relationship you have with the other party and you want to resolve the conflict in such a way that the other party is satisfied and the relationship remains intact. Parakeets are willing to accommodate others and give in to what the other person wants rather than adhere to their own point of view. "Okay, we'll do it your way" is something you will frequently hear from a Parakeet. They are at the opposite end of the grid from the Woodpecker – high on the *focus on other* side and low on the *focus on self* side.

You are an Owl if your concern for both self and other are high. In other words, Owls have a vested interest in how the conflict is resolved. Owls are not willing to simply give in to the other party. They want their perspective to be heard and understood but they also want the other party to be completely satisfied with the outcome. "Let's talk it all out" is the Owl's approach.

Ostriches are in the opposite corner of the grid. Ostriches want to avoid conflict at all costs. They do not wish to acknowledge that conflict exists and they certainly do not want to engage in conflict. Therefore they are low on the *focus on self* side of the grid as well as the *focus on other* side. Even in the midst of a conflict situation you might hear an Ostrich say "Conflict? What conflict?"

Hummingbirds fit in the middle of the grid. They have a moderate concern for self and a moderate concern for others. For this reason, Hummingbirds are often difficult for others to figure out. They seem willing to compromise somewhat on almost every aspect of a conflict. The Hummingbird's attitude seems to be "I'll give a little if you will."

Having identified your conflict management style, it's probably not difficult to understand why you use it most often. It may have been the way conflict was handled in your family when you were growing up. One of our workshop participants once told us, "I'm an Ostrich and I come by it honestly. I am descended from a long line of Ostriches!" You may realize that you handle conflict just like your mentor or your conflict management style is the only way to get things done at work. It may be a response to someone else's conflict management style. Another workshop participant told us, "For years I worked for a boss who was a Woodpecker. I never pecked back. We both knew who was the boss. The only way for me to survive was to smile and give in quickly. My Parakeet style has been reinforced over and over again in every aspect of my life."

Regardless of why or how you developed this conflict management style, it is important to understand why and how this style works for you and against you. You will gain an in-depth understanding of each conflict management style in the following chapters.

Now that you've determined your conflict management style, have a look at your second highest score. This is likely also a style that you use. What is the difference between your highest score and your second highest score? If it is less than ten, it is likely that you also use this style quite frequently. What about your third highest score? How close is it to the top two scores? If it is also within ten points of your highest score, it is also a style that you probably use regularly. The same applies to your fourth and finally your lowest score. If, however, there is significant difference between your scores, your low scores indicate a discomfort or infrequent use of that particular conflict management style.

Your scores may be very close together or very spread out. You may have several styles where your scores are very close and then one or two styles that are significantly greater or lesser. The guideline for looking at your results is that higher numbers (relative to the rest of your scores) indicate a greater preference or greater use of that style and lower scores (again, relative to the rest of your scores) indicate less preference or less use of that style.

It is important to remember as you look at your results that they are descriptive and not prescriptive. Your results describe how you tend to behave in conflict situations but they do not prescribe how you *should* behave in conflict situations. Just because you were identified as a Parakeet in the questionnaire does not mean that you always were and always will be a Parakeet in every conflict situation you are ever faced with! It simply means that you are most comfortable dealing with conflict as a Parakeet and most frequently behave as a Parakeet in conflict situations now, as things are today. You may embrace other conflict management styles in the future or may have done so in the past. In fact, you may look back on your development as a person and recall that you used to behave much more as a Hummingbird or a Woodpecker or any of the other conflict management styles. Certainly life circumstances and experiences play a part in how we tend to deal with conflict.

Remember also that you answered the questionnaire as *you* see yourself. It may be helpful to discuss your results with someone who knows you well and who you trust to be honest with you. Ask them how they have perceived your behavior in conflict situations. They may confirm your perspective or may encourage you to see yourself in a different light.

Determining your conflict management style is not intended to be an excuse for your behavior. The results of the questionnaire may, however, explain a great deal about the patterns and consequences to conflict situations that you have experienced in the past. This is an opportunity to look at some of the conflict situations that you have been involved in and ask yourself, "Was that the best possible conclusion? Could the result have been more productive?" You may discover that you are not always using your conflict management style to its best advantage or that you need to broaden your repertoire in how you deal with conflict.

By examining your past experiences with conflict, you can begin to make a more proactive choice about how you will deal with conflict in the future. Not every conflict management style is equally effective in every conflict situation. But every conflict management style has its appropriate uses. Learning to *migrate* from one style to another, depending on the conflict, will allow you to experience conflict in a more positive and constructive way.

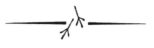

3

WOODPECKERS

Martha The Woodpecker

Martha was a very bright and successful young manager who was giving her employers the results they wanted. She was a woman who got things done. In fact, the production level in her department had increased over seventy-five percent since Martha had taken over just two years before. As far as Senior Management was concerned, she was a star employee.

One day, with no forewarning of anything amiss, Senior Management received notice of several grievances against Martha. Martha was managing twelve employees at the time. These employees had launched fourteen different complaints against Martha, accusing her of poor management skills, abuse of power, and harassment.

Martha was distraught and angry. She couldn't believe that her staff would do such a thing to her. She had been one of them just a few years ago. She had worked her way up through the ranks. She had proven herself by implementing several cost-cutting measures that had saved the company thousands of dollars. She couldn't believe that Senior Management would even consider that the allegations made by her staff could have any merit. She threatened her staff and Senior Management with lawsuits for defamation of character. She hired lawyers to defend her reputation.

The organization was stunned – not only by Martha's threat of lawsuits but also by the allegations of the employees. The fact was that Martha was very bright and had found some innovative ways to increase productivity in her department. Senior Management had noticed the results Martha was achieving. She always received positive feedback from them on her performance.

What Senior Management was not aware of was Martha's management style. According to her staff, Martha sent out weekly directives informing staff of their task assignments for the week. In this process, she had removed any opportunity for the staff to ask questions or provide feedback about client response. The previous manager had put an emphasis on building rapport with the clients. As far as the employees were concerned, Martha didn't care about rapport – with the clients or her staff.

The staff also claimed that Martha had changed their job descriptions without advance notice or discussing it with them. She took away much of their decision-making ability and yet wanted detailed reports on how they were spending their time.

One staff member overheard Martha tell another manager, "I don't get paid to be nice to people. I get paid to get the job done." The staff felt betrayed by Martha's attitude. She had been just like them until she got the promotion to manager. "It's as if she became another person when she became the manager," one staff member said.

Now her employees were calling her a tyrant. A few staff members had tried to confront Martha about their issues and concerns, but Martha had been dismissive. "If you don't like the way I do things, you can leave. I'm the boss here — it's my way or the highway." After that, employees were afraid to confront Martha because they were fearful of negative repercussions. The employees finally decided that the only way to address their concerns was to get together and file formal grievances.

Martha was a Woodpecker. In her work, she was always focused on the task and getting the job done. But in her quest to get the job done, Martha had trampled on a lot of people's feelings, egos and self-worth. She had not concerned herself with the effect her demands had on her staff. And when this caused conflict she dismissed it. As far as Martha was concerned that was "touchy-feely" stuff that had no place in the office.

When the employees decided to file formal complaints, Martha responded by threatening lawsuits. She immediately went on the offensive, pointing out her excellent track record. Every example of mismanagement or abuse of power was countered with examples of productivity increases and a better bottom line. When questioned about her staff's allegations, Martha pointed out the mistakes, weaknesses and lack of experience of each individual employee, questioning their credibility in evaluating her managerial skills.

There are certain aspects of Martha's Woodpecker style that achieved great results. The fact that Martha was singularly focused on her goals resulted in higher production. If her employees disagreed with what she wanted done or how she wanted it done, Martha simply overruled them. There was no discussion, no debate back and forth, and no exchange of perspectives. As far as Martha was concerned, that would be a waste of time.

But Martha's Woodpecker style also got her into hot water. Her employees felt devalued and demoralized. They did not believe that they were able to make any significant contribution because they could not bring forth new ideas or a fresh perspective. They believed Martha would put them down every time they tried. When they tried to discuss the difficult work environment with Martha, she told them to "live with it or leave."

The Woodpecker's Characteristics

There's good reason why we call this conflict management style the Woodpecker style. Many of the unique characteristics of this bird can also be attributed to individuals who use the Woodpecker style in dealing with conflict.

Noisy

Many homeowners find woodpeckers annoying because they will continuously peck at a drainpipe or aluminum siding or something that makes a great deal of noise. Why are they doing this? They can't get any food like they can when they peck away at the trunk of a tree. What are they trying to accomplish? Experts believe that woodpeckers frequently peck away at something simply for the noise.

People who deal with conflict like Woodpeckers are also frequently noisy. They may loudly and adamantly argue and disagree. Sometimes they may not have much of a point to make other than to state that the other party is wrong. At other times they will painstakingly and thoroughly argue their points. Often it seems that Woodpeckers do so because they enjoy the noise. It may even appear to others that the Woodpecker is arguing just for the sake of arguing. Conflict is often exciting for Woodpeckers. It's a bit of a game. They want to prove the other person wrong, score some points, and win.

Tenacious

Woodpeckers are known for their ability to cling to the trunks of trees and focus in on a spot to peck away at until they get at the insect that will be their dinner. They have a sharp, straight, chisel-shaped bill that allows them to peck at the trunk of the tree until they have burrowed a hole in the trunk. Then they use their long tongue (some types of woodpeckers even have barbs and bristles at the end of the tongue) to capture the insects inside. Reaching the goal may take the woodpecker some time, but all the while the woodpecker clings to the side of the tree without falling or losing its footing.

Those who are Woodpeckers in conflict situations are often described in similar terms. Woodpeckers will stick to a position and hammer away – making their point in the strongest way possible. Just like the barbs and bristles at the end of the bird's tongue, those who are Woodpeckers in conflict will use biting comments and criticisms to strengthen the effect of their statements. They show little or no interest in listening to the other party. They do not want to hear anything that might change their point of view. Their footing or position remains secure as they adamantly push the other party to accept their perspective.

Woodpeckers tend to exhibit *either-or* thinking. They have a strong sense of how things should be. In their opinion, anything that deviates from this is simply wrong. Woodpeckers operate under the philosophy that if someone else is wrong they should be confronted with it and corrected. The expectation, of course, is that the other party will recognize the rightness of the Woodpecker's viewpoint and simply adopt it. And if it's not that easy, well then, the Woodpecker will need to peck a little harder to get the rightness of their viewpoint across!

Single-Minded

A firefighter told us a story about woodpeckers. Apparently there are instances when, in the midst of a forest fire, firefighters have come across woodpeckers on the trunks of trees continuing to peck at the tree even when there is fire all around them. It's as if they are so focused on their task and on that point on the trunk of the tree that they are unaware of the danger around them. Even a forest fire cannot distract them from their goal!

In conflict, Woodpeckers can be the same way. They are completely focused on their task of getting the other party to give in and agree with them. They want to gain the advantage. The Woodpecker will not walk away from a confrontation when it gets heated – in fact it's the Woodpecker who is usually heating things up! Woodpeckers want results.

Conflict is seen as something that must be dealt with as swiftly and efficiently as possible. For this reason, Woodpeckers confront the conflict and those that they disagree with quickly. They do not minimize their points of disagreement or try to soften their perspective. Woodpeckers do not usually leave you wondering what they're thinking! They have little tolerance for anything or anyone that will distract them from getting the result they want.

Utilitarian

Woodpeckers are considered opportunistic birds. Not only do they peck at the trunks of trees, but they will fly out from their perch in a tree to catch insects in midair or on the ground. They will move from trunk to limb, from branch to air, or on the ground. Woodpeckers are known to use whatever movement or action is useful at the moment. They may not appear particularly graceful in their movements, but woodpeckers accomplish what they set out to do.

Those who use the Woodpecker conflict management style are equally utilitarian. Because they want to win, they are very demanding. And they will not necessarily state their demands politely or diplomatically. They will pursue their own goals at the expense of the other party.

The Woodpecker motto often seems to be "nice guys finish last." Woodpeckers, when embroiled in a conflict, are usually willing to do whatever it takes to win. If this means pointing out the weaknesses of the other party and discrediting the other person in some way, the Woodpecker will not hesitate to do so. If it means repeating a point over and over again in an attempt to wear down the other party, the Woodpecker will not hesitate to do so. If it means exerting any type of power or control over the other party, the Woodpecker will not hesitate to do so.

The Woodpecker's Tactics

Woodpeckers want to win. In order to win, they use a variety of behaviors or tactics when they find themselves involved in a conflict situation. Some Woodpeckers may use these tactics very deliberately. For others, these behaviors are more subconscious. If you are a Woodpecker, you have likely found yourself using a number of these tactics in conflict situations. If you have been in conflict with a Woodpecker, you have probably been at the receiving end of many of these behaviors. Some of the behaviors or tactics that Woodpeckers frequently use are described here.

Direct Confrontation

Woodpeckers do not shy away from conflict. If there is an issue that needs to be addressed, Woodpeckers will do so. They do not hesitate to get into a verbal confrontation. The confrontational remarks of the Woodpecker will be either assertive or aggressive.

The assertive Woodpecker doesn't berate or ridicule the other person but very stubbornly adheres to his or her position. An example of this would be the father who wants his teenage son home by a certain time.

"Have a good time. I want you home by ten o'clock."

"Ten? Come on, Dad, the party will barely be getting started. Can't I stay until midnight?"

"I want you home by ten."

"At least eleven? Everyone else will still be there."

"You're coming home at ten."

"I'll do extra chores tomorrow. Anything."

"Ten."

"Dad . . ."

"Ten!"

This type of direct confrontation puts the pressure on the other person to change. In the example above, the father continues to stick to his position – his son is to be home by ten o'clock. There is no negotiation. There is no deviation from the message. In the end, the son knows that he cannot change his father's mind and so he gives in. "Okay, I'll be home at ten."

Some Woodpeckers use direct confrontation that is much more aggressive. They use put downs to discredit the other party's position or argument. Comments like "you don't know what you're talking about" or "do your homework before you come whining to me" or "that's the stupidest thing I ever heard" are used to berate or ridicule the other person.

The purpose for these confrontational remarks, whether they are simply assertive or more aggressive, is much the same. They are used to make the Woodpecker's position clear and to demonstrate the strength of that position.

Threats And Bluffs

The Woodpecker knows that knowledge is power. Rarely will the Woodpecker share any information that would allow the other party to gain a greater understanding of the situation and thus an advantage. In fact, the Woodpecker will often deliberately attempt to put the other party at a disadvantage by maintaining a high level of secrecy.

The Woodpecker will then use threats to win the argument. To use our earlier example of the father who wants his son home by ten o'clock, this tactic would look something like this:

"Have a good time. I want you home by ten o'clock."

"Ten? Come on, Dad, the party will barely be getting started. Can't I stay until midnight?"

"If you're not home by ten, you're grounded for a week."

"Can I stay until at least eleven? Everyone else will still be there."

"Keep that up, and you're grounded for two weeks."

"I'll do extra chores tomorrow. Anything."

"Three weeks and you can't borrow the car for a month!"

Some of the Woodpecker's threats might be bluffs, but others are very real. This tactic obviously works best if the Woodpecker is in a position of power and has something to threaten the other party with. In the example above, the father has the power and authority to discipline his son by grounding him. Will he actually go to the extreme of grounding him for three weeks or is that just a bluff? It's often hard to know whether a Woodpecker is bluffing or not. But whether the threat is real or simply a bluff, this tactic creates discomfort and uncertainty in the other party.

Rejection

The Woodpecker may respond to the other party with statements that reject that person's perspective. "Oh, come on, it's not that bad" or "You don't know what you're talking about" or "You've got nothing to complain about" are the types of comments Woodpeckers will use to indicate that they are unwilling to listen to the other person's position. It can even be a simple "that's not true" in response to comments made by the other party. In this way the Woodpecker does not engage in any discussion of the other party's perspective because it has been totally negated by the Woodpecker.

In some cases a Woodpecker rejects the opinions or viewpoint of the other party by ignoring it completely. The Woodpecker doesn't say anything directly to the other party but continues to pursue his or her goal. This is often done when the Woodpecker is not the person in an authority position. To use our earlier example of the father who wants his son home by ten o'clock, if the son was the Woodpecker the conversation might go something like this:

"Have a good time. I want you home by ten o'clock."

"Ten? Come on, Dad, the party will barely be getting started."

"I want you home by ten."

And with that, the son simply leaves and does not return home by ten. Because the son has not responded any further, he has rejected his father's instruction to be home by ten o'clock. By refusing to engage in any further discussion with his father and acting on his own goals, the son believes that he has won.

The Woodpecker's Motivation

There are certain basic personal needs that are the driving force or motivation for our behavior in conflict situations. Often these needs are subconscious. They are a part of that *knee-jerk* reaction that often determines our conflict management style.

When we engage in conflict with another person who has a different conflict management style than our own, we often wonder at their behavior. We question what they are expecting to accomplish by their actions or communication style. We see them as difficult, unreasonable, or unrealistic. But it is important to consider the other party's motivation. We need to understand what is driving that behavior. We need to recognize, in a very fundamental way, *why* that person is behaving in that way. If you are in conflict with someone who is a Woodpecker, understanding the motivation for his or her behavior means you are better equipped to deal with that person.

Respect

Woodpeckers want to be recognized as having something valuable to say. They want to have their point of view validated by others. What the Woodpecker is looking for is respect. Woodpeckers want their thoughts and options to be held in high regard. They want to be listened to.

For Woodpeckers, agreement is often interpreted as respect. They see disagreement or even questioning as signs of disrespect. When the Woodpecker's argument is questioned, the Woodpecker becomes agitated and annoyed. This usually results in the escalation of the Woodpecker's tactics. Woodpeckers will then become increasingly adamant and will stubbornly adhere to their positions. By their behavior, Woodpeckers are trying to demand respect – even insisting on it!

To Be Right

Woodpeckers are insistent that their way is the right way. They can't stand the thought of being wrong. Being wrong would leave the Woodpecker open to criticism.

Interestingly, the Woodpecker's desire to be right is so overwhelming that the Woodpecker will often continue to argue the point even when confronted with clear evidence that it's wrong.

There is an old Arabic saying that, translated, goes something like this: *even if it flies, it's a goat.* A story we were once told is a perfect example of this need to maintain a position no matter what. There was a very proud and stubborn man. He did not like dissent and life was either good or bad, right or wrong. Gray areas did not exist. Rarely was he challenged about his thoughts or ideas because people did not want to get on his bad side. So he lived most of his life thinking he was right. One day, in the midst of a debate about the current political situation, this man's grandson noticed that his grandfather was wrong. The grandson didn't just disagree with his grandfather's opinion, but he recognized that some of the factual information that his grandfather was relating was incorrect. The grandson interrupted his grandfather. "But Grandfather, I read in this book that the facts are actually something else." For the Woodpecker grandfather, this criticism was unacceptable. He pointed out his superior knowledge in the subject matter, his life experience, and the fact that he was well read in world affairs. But the grandson knew that his grandfather was wrong. As much as the grandson pushed the grandfather to admit that he was mistaken on his facts, the grandfather refused. The grandson kept asking his grandfather "But grandfather, how can you say that when I can prove that it is not so?" The grandfather's reply was "It is so because I said it is so."

Attention

Remember the Woodpecker that pecks at the drainpipe just for the noise? Many Woodpeckers are attention-seekers. They enjoy a good confrontation because it focuses attention on them.

Not all Woodpeckers will purposefully pick a fight just for the attention. But most Woodpeckers will fiercely confront someone and strongly state their position even when the issue is not particularly important to them.

A friend gave us a good example of this from her own experience. Mary was eating dinner in a busy restaurant. When asked whether she would like the soup or salad with her meal, Mary requested the soup. The busy waiter, however, mistakenly brought Mary a salad. Mary reminded the waiter that she wanted the soup, which he promised to bring right out. He didn't bring it out. And before long, Mary received her dinner without being served the soup. Again, Mary made a point of telling the waiter that she had not received her soup. He once again promised to bring it out. When it was still not forthcoming, Mary demanded to speak to the manager to have the situation addressed. Later Mary admitted that her insistence on the matter was not because she was hungry for the soup. She wanted the matter addressed because she felt ignored when she did not get what she had ordered. Even though the soup was not particularly important to her, Mary was determined to make some noise and get the restaurant's attention.

What To Expect When You're A Woodpecker

When you use the Woodpecker conflict management style appropriately, your motivational needs are met. As a Woodpecker you will get the attention and respect you want and deserve. However, if you are a Woodpecker in all conflict situations, or in inappropriate situations, there are frequently negative consequences. The *constant* use of the Woodpecker style will not give you the results you desire. Here are some of the results you can expect when you use the Woodpecker style exclusively.

Alienation And Anger

Woodpecker behavior, especially when used consistently, results in the isolation of the Woodpecker. The Woodpecker is focused on the goal and achieving a win. This results in a *me-them* mentality. There is no opportunity to work together with the other party to find a resolution to the conflict. The Woodpecker sees everyone as an adversary – someone to score points on, to play against. Woodpeckers become alienated from those around them. For the Woodpecker there is a clear sense of needing to go it alone.

The Woodpecker doesn't always come up against someone who is willing to give in. In other words, the Woodpecker doesn't always win. When this happens, the Woodpecker usually gets angry. This anger, in turn, intensifies the Woodpecker's behavior and makes the Woodpecker more aggressive and even hostile.

Negative Stereotypes

Woodpeckers need to be right. Consequently, in their opinion, anyone Woodpeckers come into conflict with is wrong. When a Woodpecker experiences a great deal of conflict it can seem to the Woodpecker that no one ever does anything right. Not only does this add to the Woodpecker's sense of alienation, it leads to negative stereotypes. In extreme cases, Woodpeckers come to view everyone who questions them as "stupid" or "slow" or "foolish."

At the same time, when the Woodpecker wins the fight, the Woodpecker sees the opponent as weak and easily defeated. Woodpeckers then form negative stereotypes of those they are in conflict with as not being able to stand up for themselves and not being committed to their viewpoint.

Defensiveness

For those who find themselves in conflict with a Woodpecker there can be a feeling of being dominated and controlled. Because the Woodpecker is forceful, the other party feels pushed around by the Woodpecker. The Woodpecker's confrontational style makes the other party feel defensive. In this situation, the other party is tempted to combat the threats and attacks of the Woodpecker. When the Woodpecker uses these tactics, the attacks and threats may have very little to do with the actual issue causing the conflict. The other party then feels that they are trying to fend off an ambush because they don't know which direction the next attack will come from. In fact, the real issue that was at the heart of the conflict may become lost in the fray.

Conflict Escalation

Janet and Steve, a young couple out on a date, disagreed on what movie they should see. Janet, a Woodpecker, simply ignored Steve's opinion and purchased tickets for the movie she wanted to see while Steve was at the concession stand. When Steve expressed displeasure over Janet's choice of movie, her reaction was a sarcastic "Have you read the reviews for that other movie?" Before long, Janet was making comments regarding Steve's limited interests, his inability to make decisions, and his unwillingness to try new things. Within minutes, Janet was threatening, "I don't think I can continue to see someone who is so narrow-minded." In using these tactics, Janet elevated the conflict to something that was no longer about which movie to see.

When the Woodpecker style is used excessively, the conflict is likely to escalate. Because the Woodpecker uses a number of confrontational and aggressive tactics, the other party can get caught up in addressing those attacks. What began as a relatively minor or simple disagreement may evolve into a major crisis.

A Winner And A Loser

When Woodpeckers are involved in conflict, the end result is that someone wins and someone loses. Woodpeckers will, of course, make every attempt to come out the winner. The other party is then automatically the loser. If the Woodpeckers cannot clearly win the argument, they will make every effort to make sure the other party loses. In other words, they will find any weaknesses they can and utilize those to make the other party look bad. If the other party loses then the Woodpecker declares himself the winner.

When Woodpeckers are involved in a conflict and do not get the desired result, even when achieving some of what they want, Woodpeckers consider themselves to have lost. But beware. Most Woodpeckers who have lost will come back to fight the same fight another day!

When To Be A Woodpecker

Because our conflict management style is usually a reflex reaction rather than a planned response, we frequently use our conflict management style inappropriately– with negative results. But every conflict management style can be useful in certain situations. Below are several types of conflict situations where the Woodpecker style can be used appropriately and successfully.

When Responding To Crisis Situations

When a house is burning down the homeowners don't want the fire chief to have a collaborative conversation with the rest of the firefighters to determine who should do what. "You seemed a little uncomfortable last time with taking the front of the hose…maybe we should do it differently this time, what do you think?" The house could burn down in the mean time! The fire chief needs to order people into place with little or no consultation or hesitation. He is in charge and everyone knows it and follows orders whether they agree at the moment or not.

There are those situations where your disagreement with the other party is not up for discussion. A quick and decisive response is essential. The parent who sees her child playing with matches will shout, "Stop that!" and grab the matches away. She doesn't pause first to explore why the child wants to play with matches or to explain why she disagrees with the child's current activity.

Utilizing the Woodpecker style in this type of emergency situation does not negate the need to potentially discuss the situation later. The parent will need to discuss safety and explain why playing with matches can be dangerous at some point. If the fire crew is not fighting fires efficiently the chief will need to address who does what at the scene of a fire. But this needs to happen at a later time, when the crisis is over. In the midst of an emergency, the Woodpecker style is appropriate.

When You Must Enforce The Rules

Parents frequently have to tell their children that they cannot do something they really want to do – like eating a handful of candy right before dinner. No matter how many times they ask, whine, pout, or argue about it the answer is always the same – no.

Some rules or actions are unpopular but non-negotiable. There may be individuals who disagree with what those rules are and their disagreement is disruptive. If you are the person who is responsible for enforcing those rules you may need to act like a Woodpecker to do so.

When Dealing With Critical Issues

There are many conflict situations when you know you are right but it simply isn't worth arguing about. However, when you know you're right and the issue is of vital importance, you may need to behave like a Woodpecker and stick to your position no matter what. This includes those strongly held values that you are unwilling to compromise.

History pays tribute to individuals from Gandhi to Martin Luther King who held such deep commitment to a principle that they were not willing to compromise it in any way. These individuals acted like Woodpeckers in this respect. Although they were nonviolent, they were confrontational. Their positions were deeply rooted in their personal values and they did not back down from their positions in the face of adversity or criticism. The tenacity of these individuals resulted in movements, changes, and new ways of thinking that are of historical significance.

You Don't Have To Be A Woodpecker All The Time

If you find yourself overusing or misusing the Woodpecker conflict management style you have likely experienced some of the negative consequences of your behavior. You need to look for ways to move beyond your Woodpecker style. But, because behaving like a Woodpecker is such an automatic response to conflict for you, there are some things you need to consider in order to change your behavior.

Consider The Other Person

Who are you in conflict with? What is your relationship with that person? How will that relationship be impacted by your behavior? Sometimes you need a relationship to remain intact. Frequently, Woodpecker behavior causes relationships to weaken or even dissolve. If the relationship is important to you in the long term, then the Woodpecker style of dealing with conflict may not be appropriate for achieving that goal.

Consider The Need For Buy In

Do you need the other party to truly *buy in* to your idea? The Woodpecker style demands agreement from the other party. This does not necessarily mean that the other party is committed to the Woodpecker's point of view. They may simply be agreeing for purposes of self-preservation. If you need the other party to be truly committed to your perspective, you will need to do more than *force* them to agree.

Listen

Make sure you understand what the other party is saying before you respond. Woodpeckers rarely take the time to listen to the other party's perspective. Ask yourself if you know what it is that the other party needs or wants. Then ask them if what you heard them say is what they really meant. Make sure that you are not making assumptions about the other party's position but have truly heard what that person is trying to communicate.

Identify The Issues

Clearly identify the issues in the conflict. What are the actual points you don't agree on? Once you have identified the issues, determine which ones are negotiable and which are non-negotiable to you. In other words, prioritize the issues. Are there some that are not important to you? Are there others that are more important? Are there any issues that you have particularly strong feelings about and are completely unwilling to consider a compromise on? If so, try to figure out why those issues are so important to you. Then explain your perspective to the other party.

Pause Before Responding

You've heard it said that you should count to ten before you say something in anger, right? This is critical advice for the Woodpecker. Because Woodpeckers are so quick to jump into a confrontation, their choice of words may be abrupt, rude, overly critical or exaggerated. If you're a Woodpecker, consider your words and whether or not they truly reflect the message you wish to get across.

Tips For Dealing With Woodpeckers

All of us have come in contact with Woodpeckers at some time or other. Whether that person is using the Woodpecker style in an appropriate way or not, there are some things that are important to keep in mind so that you can deal with that Woodpecker and not end up feeling dominated, controlled or defensive.

Communicate

First and foremost, don't withdraw. It is tempting for many to simply turn around and walk away when the party you are in conflict with becomes overly assertive or aggressive. But to Woodpeckers, withdrawing can be seen as a weakness that they can then take advantage of.

If at all possible, keep communication open. Maintain dialogue. Listen to what the Woodpecker has to say. The Woodpecker's communication style may be critical. Ignore personal attacks but acknowledge constructive criticism. You may need to sift through what the Woodpecker says. Don't get sidetracked by the Woodpecker's noise. Listen for the valid points the Woodpecker makes and focus on them.

Frequently Woodpeckers simply need time to have their say. Even though it may not be done in the most constructive way, give Woodpeckers time to get it out of their system. Allow Woodpeckers to talk and make their position clear before you join the debate.

Ask Questions

Rather than becoming defensive and giving explanations for your position, ask questions about why the Woodpecker sees it a different way. Ask for clarity on the Woodpecker's position – why do they see their way as the best resolution? What might be the long-term results of the Woodpecker's position? But remember, when asking these questions the intent is to understand the Woodpecker's point of view, not find fault with their reasoning. As much as you can, model curiosity and a desire to understand.

Use Self-Assertive Language

Be clear about your position. Don't try to hedge or sugarcoat what you say. Be direct and unambiguous about what you have to contribute, what you think and why you have this position. Avoid inflammatory or emotional words – it's far too tempting for the Woodpecker to pick up on these and use them to make the argument more personal.

It is important that you talk about the conflict from your perspective. Use statements such as "the way I see it" or "this is how I feel about the situation" rather than "you aren't being fair" or "you think that…" Use "I" statements rather than statements that make assumptions about the Woodpecker's position. When you use "you" statements the Woodpecker will feel a need to defend or rebut these statements. The conflict can then be easily sidetracked or it can escalate.

Don't Get Drawn In

When a Woodpecker *attacks* (and that's the right word because it often feels like an attack) it is important not to immediately get drawn into this communication pattern. Direct and immediate retaliation will rarely be successful because you will not be prepared, especially if you were not anticipating the confrontation.

It can be appropriate to reschedule the discussion and give yourself time to prepare. Make sure you know what your position is and that you have your emotions under control. When it is time to confront that Woodpecker you might want to do so in private. Remember that one of the needs of the Woodpecker is attention. If your confrontation has an audience, it will be much more difficult for the Woodpecker to go beyond posturing.

Allow The Woodpecker To Save Face

Even if you need to assert yourself with a Woodpecker, don't get drawn in to making personal attacks or trying to embarrass or discredit the Woodpecker. This will only enhance the fighting mood of the Woodpecker and won't get you anywhere. The only way you will see movement from a Woodpecker and potentially have a constructive dialogue is to allow the Woodpecker to save face. This does not mean giving in or letting the Woodpecker score points at your expense. It does mean maintaining open communication, focusing on anything constructive the Woodpecker has to say, and making sure that the Woodpecker has a chance to state her position. In doing so you will be allowing the Woodpecker to save face.

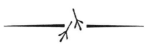

4

PARAKEETS

Doug The Parakeet

Doug had been brought in to ITR Technologies by the CEO four years ago to develop the market analysis division. He remembered when the division consisted of himself and his assistant. Now he was the director of a division with a staff of almost fifty. The company had recognized the market analysis division for its exemplary work. In his office, Doug displayed the many commendations the division had received.

At a meeting of his division managers, Doug announced a new project that they had just been awarded. He was surprised by their lack of enthusiasm for the new project. He had expected them to be excited about the challenge and the opportunity to further expand the division's areas of expertise. Instead, they erupted. They pointed out weaknesses in the project. They argued about who should be doing what. Several of the managers questioned the validity of the project itself. Doug was frustrated and he didn't know what to do. He couldn't understand why his staff couldn't be more positive about the project and more supportive of each other. He was expecting the managers to engage in a brainstorming session where they would put together a plan for the project and assign key responsibilities. This did not happen.

When Doug arrived at the office the next day his assistant, Celine, said she had heard about the explosion at the managers' meeting. She wanted to know what had happened.

"Oh, it wasn't that bad. I wouldn't call it an explosion," said Doug. "Everything will be fine. Everybody just needs a little time to digest all the information they were given yesterday."

Concerned that the last meeting and the project were going to be the topic of negative gossip, Doug called another managers' meeting for the end of the week. He decided he needed to drum up a little more excitement about the project in order to get the managers going in a more positive direction. He put together a stunning visual presentation highlighting the benefits of the project – for the company, the division, and the individuals involved in the project. He expressed his personal interest in the project and assured the managers of his complete support. He still didn't get the response he was hoping for.

"Maybe they felt overwhelmed by the scope of the project," Doug thought. He decided he needed to break it down into more manageable pieces. For the next week Doug worked day and night to put together initial research and to develop a project plan. He determined key responsibilities. Rather than call another managers' meeting, Doug assigned staff to various tasks individually.

Doug also asked several staff to complete some key reports for him by the next Friday. He gave them very clear and specific guidelines for the reports because they were vital to the project. When the reports were handed in, Doug felt they were incomplete. In one case, he was certain that some of the information put into the report was actually incorrect. Doug was tempted to ask that the reports be redone but he knew that it was difficult for the staff that had worked on the reports to put in any extra time over the weekend. He needed the reports for Monday. Doug decided to redo the reports himself, working the entire weekend to have them completed by Monday.

The next week Sandra, one of the managers who had initially objected to the project, approached Doug and asked why she had not been assigned any responsibilities for the project. Doug was surprised by Sandra's sudden interest in the project but he simply apologized for the oversight. Doug decided to rework the assignments and included Sandra in the project team.

At the next managers' meeting, the managers were agitated. The managers who were not involved in the project were angry. They told Doug that he should have given them all an equal opportunity to get involved. They accused him of playing favorites as he assigned tasks. They used words like "secretive" and "biased" and "unfair." Doug was extremely upset by their comments and was tempted to remind them of their negative reaction to the project at that first meeting, but he didn't. Instead, he reassured them that there was still plenty to do and everyone could be involved.

As a Parakeet, Doug liked to think of his division as a team that was more like a family – but a family that got along, not one that argued all of the time! He was extremely upset by the negativity of the managers. They seemed unwilling to work cooperatively and seemed suspicious of everyone else's motives. But Doug didn't want to think badly of his staff. He tried to be understanding and look for reasons behind their actions – maybe they didn't understand what they were supposed to do, maybe his direction wasn't clear, maybe their workload was too stressful.

Doug tried to alleviate any further outbursts or hurt feelings by addressing all the possible reasons for the negativity in the workplace. He explained assignments in detail, he took more work upon himself in order to lighten some of the staff's workload, and he constantly asked staff if they understood what was being asked of them. Unfortunately, Doug's helping was wreaking havoc on his staff. They resented what they saw as interfering, and their sense of inadequacy and ineffectiveness increased.

The Parakeet's Characteristics

There is a reason why people like Doug are called Parakeets. Many of their behaviors in conflict situations parallel the characteristics of this type of bird.

Friendly

Parakeets are friendly birds. They are, in fact, the bird most commonly kept as a pet. They are cheerful, happy and active birds that respond well to other birds and to people. They are quite willing to sit on your shoulder or finger. They are not difficult to handle and don't tend to nip at people or act temperamental in any way.

Those who deal with conflict in the Parakeet style are similar in that they tend to be friendly and don't want to ruffle any feathers. Parakeets are rarely seen as difficult people because they don't usually verbalize their disagreement with others. If they do disagree and are able to tell others that they disagree, they will do so with a smile on their face and as gently as possible!

Talkative

Parakeets are excellent talkers, having the ability to mimic many sounds. When these birds are spoken to in a conversational tone, they will chirp back pleasantly. Some parakeets, in fact, will chirp back with sounds very close to human speech.

People who adopt a Parakeet conflict management style also tend to be very talkative. They know how to use pleasantries and chitchat to make others more comfortable and at ease. In conflict, Parakeets will use this ability and talk about the positive aspects of the situation. They will often say what they think the other party wants to hear. They are more likely to focus on the points of agreement rather than on the points of disagreement. Consequently, for those in conflict with Parakeets it may appear that the Parakeet is unaware of the gravity of the situation. This is not necessarily the case. For many Parakeets, the more serious the conflict, the more they talk. But they will talk around the issue – talking about almost everything and often the most inconsequential things, rather than the main points of contention.

Relationship-Oriented

Experts on bird behavior say that parakeets are birds that need a family – whether they are domesticated or live in the wild. They are considered loyal animals. Domestic parakeets bond with their owners and respond positively to that connection. In the wild, they live in groups, seemingly because they need the interaction and the social connection.

Those who deal with conflict like Parakeets also need relationships. They value contact and are concerned about how conflict will affect their interactions with others. Many Parakeets believe that if they argue or disagree with someone they will be viewed negatively by that person. Consequently, Parakeets will often ignore their own needs or concerns in order to accommodate the needs of the other party.

Agreeable

Parakeets are very agreeable birds. They are rarely seen fighting with other birds – either of their own species or other species. They are extremely adaptable to their surroundings, responding positively to changes in their environment.

Those who use the Parakeet conflict management style are also very agreeable. They are always striving for harmony, trying to please the other party. They don't enjoy conflict and find it difficult to consider that there could be any positive benefits to conflict. Parakeets see potential conflict and do whatever they can to circumvent direct disagreement. When conflict does happen, Parakeets are likely to be the ones to give in to the other party in order to maintain harmony.

The Parakeet's Tactics

Many Parakeets will say that they do not experience a great deal of conflict. This is because they are focused on maintaining a sense of peace and harmony. When they see the potential for conflict they try to make sure that it does not result in a direct confrontation.

Parakeets want to keep the peace. This means keeping the other party happy. Consequently the Parakeet will use a variety of tactics to make sure that everyone gets along.

Here are some of the most common tactics or behaviors used by Parakeets.

Gloss Over The Situation

Parakeets, when faced with possible conflict, will frequently gloss over the most contentious issues. They may not give all the facts, or present the situation in such a way that it doesn't appear as serious, in order to play down the negative.

Ted had an assigned parking spot in the parking lot adjacent to his apartment building. One evening when he got home from work another car was parked in his space. Ted was irritated by the inconvenience but assumed the car owner had not seen the "Assigned Parking Only" sign. He parked on the street that evening. But when this happened for several more evenings, Ted became very annoyed and no longer believed that the car owner had simply missed the sign.

On the third evening, Ted knew he had to do something about the car in his parking spot. He knew that he could call the building superintendent and they would have the car towed away. But Ted felt that this course of action was too serious. Ted decided to write a note to the owner of the car. He was sure if he just told the owner of the car that this was an assigned spot and he could not park there, everything would be taken care of.

Ted, a Parakeet, wrote the following note and placed it on the windshield of the car.

Dear Sir/Madam:

You may not be aware of this but the spot you are currently parked in is an assigned spot. Parking for guests or those without assigned spots is available in the adjacent parking lot or on the street. I am sure that you did not realize this when you parked here and did not intend to inconvenience anyone but, in the future, would you mind parking in another location? Your cooperation is greatly appreciated.

Notice that Ted's note makes no reference to the fact that it was *his* parking spot the other person had parked in. The note is very friendly and helpful. There is no sense of Ted's annoyance or frustration at not being able to park in his spot. Ted assumes the best in the other party's actions – that the car owner did not know it was assigned parking and that he did not intentionally park in Ted's spot.

Cajole Or Coax

Parakeets will also attempt to coax the other person out of the conflict.

Darla knew that something was bothering her husband Kevin. All day he had been cross and overly critical of her. It seemed he was just spoiling for a fight. Darla believed that Kevin's mood was due to the fact that he had spent the previous evening paying bills. Darla knew she had made some purchases over the past month that Kevin would consider frivolous. He was always concerned about their tight budget. Darla, on the other hand, saw her purchases as adding to their quality of life without being overly extravagant.

All day, whenever Kevin made a negative comment, Darla would counter it with a positive one.

"I don't see why we need all this stuff," Kevin said.

"But it really adds to the comfortable feel of the room, doesn't it?" Darla replied.

Later, Kevin said, "I don't think we'll be able to afford that vacation next month like we talked about."

And Darla responded with, "Well, we've waited this long. We can wait a little longer."

As they were driving later that day, Kevin stated, "I wish we could just get a new car. This one is a money guzzler. It always seems to need repairs."

"Well, at least we have a car that works," Darla said. "Jim and Laura's car broke down last week and the mechanic says it's not worth fixing. They've been taking the bus ever since."

This sort of thing went on for most of the day. Finally, at dinner Kevin spoke to Darla about what was bothering him. She had been right. He believed that she was spending money without consideration for how much stress it put on their budget. He kept telling Darla how unnecessary her purchases were. She kept explaining why she thought they were necessary. He said that she needed to budget better. She said that budgets were guidelines, not absolute rules. The argument went on for several minutes with both Kevin and Darla becoming more emotional and tense. Finally Darla, a Parakeet, couldn't stand the fact that they were arguing anymore.

"I hate it when we fight. Can't we just forget this and start over? I know next month will be better. We'll budget better and I'll be more careful about my spending, I promise."

When faced with conflict, Parakeets will make every effort to cajole or coax the other party into agreement. For Darla, this meant countering the negative statements Kevin made with more positive ones. This is often done in a gentle, almost teasing way because the last thing the Parakeet wants to do is prolong the confrontation. Parakeets will often remind the other party of how good things really are, relative to how bad they might be.

Parakeets will also try to resolve conflict by pointing out the fact that they don't want to continue the conflict. Parakeets will use statements such as "I hate it when we fight" or "we don't need to argue about this, do we?" or "this isn't worth fighting about" in order to end the confrontation.

Martyrdom

Sophie kept complaining about how much stress she was under. She talked about the amount of overtime she spent. She was usually the first one in the office in the morning and the last one out at night, many times working into the wee hours of the morning.

Sophie was the manager of a really talented staff. When a colleague questioned her about her feelings of being overworked, Sophie explained her situation.

"My staff is a lot younger than I am," she said. "I know they've all got families. I'm newly single and my children are all on their own. I have less personal and family commitments. Whatever they don't get done, I finish. Sometimes they hand in sloppy work and I need to fix it. If I gave it back to them to fix I know they'd complain about the extra time. They need to spend time with their families. Rather than confront them with their mistakes and require them to put in extra time to fix it, it's just easier if I do it myself."

When her colleague probed a little further she found out that Sophie was taking care of an ailing mother, that her friends were complaining about how little time she had available for them and that she hadn't taken a vacation in years. While it was true that she didn't have a spouse or young children to care for, she didn't really have fewer social and family commitments. But she was denying that her commitments were as important as those of her staff. She accommodated their demands at the expense of her own well being in order to smooth over any awkward or difficult conversations she might need to have about the quality of their work.

Parakeets frequently downplay their own needs as unimportant compared to the needs of others. Parakeets do this because they believe that preserving the relationship is far more important than attending to their own needs.

Giving Up/Giving In

In order to keep the peace, Parakeets are likely to give in to the other party. "Whatever you want" comes to their lips quickly so that the conflict can be smoothed over. In fact, many Parakeets anticipate disagreement from another party and give in to what they perceive as the other's position before the conflict ever comes to the fore.

Monica's story is an example of this. Monica was invited to go on a weekend holiday with her friend Nancy. She was delighted with the opportunity to get away but immediately thought of her husband Mike. A few months ago when she talked to him about attending a weekend crafts course he expressed extreme annoyance with her bad timing and asked why she had to take up a whole weekend.

Monica imagined that Mike would resent her going away and leaving him at home to play chauffeur for their active children. In anticipation of this perceived conflict, Monica declined Nancy's invitation and stayed home without ever telling Mike about the opportunity.

The problem with this type of scenario is that Monica really didn't know how Mike would respond. He might have been supportive of Monica's desire to get away. He might have enjoyed the weekend alone with his children. His frustration on the previous occasion may have had nothing to do with Monica's leaving him home alone with the children. Monica made an assumption about Mike's position and gave in to it without ever hearing Mike's point of view.

The Parakeet's Motivation

It's not too difficult to understand what motivates Parakeets to behave as they do. As with the other conflict management styles, those who are Parakeets have basic personal needs that they are trying to meet by their behavior.

And, as with the other conflict management styles, when Parakeets use this style appropriately, their basic personal needs are met. However, when this style is used inappropriately or in excess, the results are frequently the opposite of what the Parakeet wants.

Let's look at the motivation behind the Parakeet's behavior.

Connection

Parakeets need to know that they are valued and that the relationship between parties is significant. This is not only true for conflicts with family and friends but any conflict the Parakeet experiences. For the Parakeet it is important that even a relative stranger not see the Parakeet as mean, rude, or difficult. Parakeets need to feel connected with others. Arguments and conflict, in the Parakeet's mind, jeopardize a relationship. "Maybe the other person will think poorly of me if I disagree or if I push for what I want" is the underlying assumption for Parakeets.

Harmony

Parakeets are greatly distressed by conflict because of their significant need for harmony. Parakeets have a very clear sense that conflict is destructive and are keenly aware of the emotional involvement that they and others have in conflict situations.

This is why Parakeets can, at times, be mistaken for Ostriches. When Parakeets are trying to smooth things over it does sometimes seem that they are avoiding the conflict. Parakeets try to anticipate possible conflict and accommodate what they perceive to be the other's position. If you ask Parakeets if they experience a great deal of conflict, they will likely say they do not.

A participant in one of our workshops once told us that she wasn't quite sure why she was there. "I never experience conflict," she said.

"You never have disagreements with your colleagues at work?" we asked.

"No. I get along great with everyone I work with," she responded.

"What about at home?"

"My husband and I have never had a fight," she said.

At this point this woman sounded like an Ostrich, not acknowledging conflict in any way. However, with a few more pointed questions, she did admit that she frequently had differences of opinions at work. But her typical response in those situations was "Oh well, if that's what it takes to get along with them I guess I can let it go." And at home, she often did look at things differently than her husband. But, as she said, most things they didn't see eye to eye on meant more to her husband than to her so she didn't want to argue about it. This woman was not an Ostrich but a Parakeet who was striving for harmony.

What To Expect When You're A Parakeet

The Parakeet conflict management style can have positive results when used appropriately. It can result in the connection and harmony that is desired by Parakeets. However, if you use this style in every conflict situation that you encounter, there can be some negative consequences.

Powerlessness

Parakeets will not assert themselves in a conflict. They are more comfortable concerning themselves with the other party's point of view rather than their own. They will yield to the other party in order to maintain a harmonious relationship. Parakeets may give in gladly or grudgingly. In either case Parakeets will feel powerless.

Parakeets may be so focused on accommodating the other party that they are not completely aware of their own emotions, views or values. In other words, Parakeets are so determined to give in to what others want that they lose sight of what they want themselves. This lack of self-awareness can result in low self-confidence.

Parakeets are frequently taken for granted. Because they are willing to go along with the wishes of the other party it is assumed that they will continue to do so. Those who have long relationships with Parakeets assume that the Parakeet will always agree with them. They don't even consider the possibility of disagreement. The Parakeet may become resentful of this expectation to constantly accommodate the other party especially if the Parakeet's contribution is not acknowledged or valued.

Because a harmonious relationship is so important to Parakeets, they usually find it difficult to see any other options other than to give in to the other party. Many Parakeets become resigned to the fact that that's just the way things are. This increases the Parakeet's sense of powerlessness.

Loss Of Respect

Those who frequently experience conflict with Parakeets talk about losing respect for them. Because Parakeets do not assert their own perspective, they seem to let people walk all over them. It may appear as if the other party could demand almost anything and the Parakeet would agree. When Parakeets are unwilling to confront someone with their own opinions, Parakeets are seen as weak and ineffective.

There is another aspect of the Parakeet's behavior that can result in a loss of respect. Many feel that the Parakeet is trying to play on their guilt. When the Parakeet says, "Okay, have it your way" the other party may feel that what the Parakeet is really saying is "look at how cooperative and obliging I am and see how stubborn and inflexible you are." Rather than appreciating the fact that the Parakeet is so willing to accommodate, the other party may feel manipulated by the Parakeet's behavior. They see the Parakeet's behavior as unfair and overly controlling.

Weak Relationships

When a Parakeet is involved in a conflict situation, the communication is pretty one-sided. There is very little back and forth dialogue. A demand or statement of some sort is made and the Parakeet adjusts or accommodates to meet the demand. Or the Parakeet anticipates the potential of conflict and gives in to the perceived needs of the other party before there is any confrontation. In such a situation there is little or no communication.

Without dialogue there is never an opportunity to really work through a conflict together. And without working through conflict together, a relationship is never allowed to grow and strengthen. What the Parakeet wants most – a harmonious relationship – is threatened by the Parakeet's behavior because, if a relationship never acknowledges and deals with conflict, it cannot flourish.

Anne gave us a powerful example of this when she told us of the demise of her 20-year marriage. She grew up, she said, in a time when her own expectations for her life were that she would get married, have babies, and care for her home and family. She did, in fact, get married at a relatively young age, had three children, and spent many happy years taking care of her family.

When she talked about how she and her husband handled the conflict in their relationship she said, "We lived by the policy that you should never let the sun set on your anger." What usually resulted when they had a disagreement was her trying to make some sort of conciliatory move towards her husband after she had been dealt the silent treatment for the better part of a day. It always went according to pattern, she said. "I would tell him that I hated it when we fought and that I didn't want us to be angry with each other. If whatever it was that we were fighting about was what he really wanted, then that's what we should do."

When the children were school age, Anne took a part time job as a teaching assistant. This eventually led to a full time job in the local school. As her children grew up and left home, Anne started to listen to some of her colleagues who told her she should be pursuing a teaching career and she should go back to school to get her degree. She was still young enough to have a full and productive career as a teacher and, with more time on her hands, she decided that this was something she wanted to do.

Her husband, however, was not excited about the prospect. The closest university was several hundred miles away and she was proposing a commuter situation for the next couple of years while she pursued her degree. "For the first time that I can remember," she said, "I didn't back down when he told me he didn't think it was a good idea. I did think it was a good idea and I reminded him of all the times I had made sacrifices for him and his career choices and now I was going to do something for myself. He was surprised at how stubborn I was. I'm sure he expected me to back down. He didn't believe I was really going to go until I got in the car and drove off that fall. Even then, I think he figured I'd try it, realize how difficult it would be to maintain our relationship, and come home. But I didn't. Over the Christmas break we had a real blow up. We'd never argued like that before. I had never yelled back but I did this time. We decided to separate after Christmas. I was a little stunned. If you had asked me just a year before, I would have said we had a great relationship that could withstand anything. We agreed on so many things. I thought the fact that we didn't argue was a sign of the strength of our relationship. Now I think it was our greatest weakness."

A Loser And A Winner

When there is a conflict and one party takes on the behaviors of a Parakeet there is a definite winner and a definite loser. And the Parakeet is always the loser. For the sake of maintaining a harmonious relationship, the Parakeet is willing to declare the other party the winner.

But there are additional losses. Parakeets may have good ideas or their perspective may be the right one but if they are unwilling to assert

themselves and confront the other party, the idea or perspective is lost. Parakeets, however, are not always willing to acknowledge this because Parakeets will often say that if we can just all get along we all win. The question is, at what expense?

When To Be A Parakeet

There are appropriate situations for using the Parakeet style. Many people will report that they utilize Parakeet behavior much more frequently at home than they do at work. Since the driving force for the Parakeet's behavior is maintaining relationships, this would make sense.

Here are some guidelines for the appropriate use of the Parakeet style.

When The Relationship Is Important

We may find ourselves in relationships where speaking up and disagreeing may have negative consequences. Take for example, the employee who disagrees with the decision to play golf at the next staff outing. She doesn't particularly enjoy golf and would prefer a different activity. Yet, if she voiced her opinion when everyone else is eager to play golf, she could be perceived as demanding and unwilling to be a team player. Here, maintaining a positive relationship with her co-workers is more important than her desire to challenge the agenda for the staff outing. So, rather than argue, she simply gives in to the group's wishes.

When we are in conflict with someone that we have a significant relationship with, the Parakeet style is sometimes the best to use. One older gentleman told us that in his thirty-nine years of marriage, the one thing that he had learned is that "yes, dear" is often the right answer! Although he said this in jest, it is true that sometimes our relationship is so important that some things are just not worth fighting about. Note that we said *some* things are not worth fighting about. Unfortunately, a true Parakeet often finds it difficult to differentiate between those things that aren't worth fighting about and those things that are.

When The Outcome Isn't Important

Some people like to argue just for the sake of arguing. They will take the opposing position just for the opportunity to have a verbal confrontation or a battle of wills. But it is important to know how to pick your battles. Sometimes what we may perceive as an occasion for playing devil's advocate may be a situation that is tremendously significant to the other party. When you find yourself in a conflict situation, consider how important the outcome is to you. If it really isn't that important to you but it is important to the other party, taking a Parakeet approach to the situation may be a good idea.

When You Need To Build Social Credits

Relationships are based on the attitude of give and take. Sometimes you take more than you give and sometimes you have to give more than you take. When you have a conflict with someone and willingly give in to them, you build good will and a sense of reciprocity. The next time you have a disagreement, they may be willing to do things your way because they experienced your willingness to do things their way last time.

Phil told us about the best employer he ever had. She knew, he said, that you catch more flies with honey than with vinegar! She would listen to ideas her staff had and, although she didn't always agree, she would allow the employee to run with their idea and try to make it work. And, Phil said, that employer had the complete loyalty of her entire staff. As Phil said, they would do anything for her because she had been willing to support them.

When You're Wrong

It can be hard to let go of an argument. Even when faced with the fact that you are not right, it can be difficult to admit it. But sometimes you're just wrong and you need to acknowledge it and move on. Parakeet behavior at this point is extremely valid. It is also an opportunity to show that you can be reasonable and learn from your mistakes.

When Others Need To Learn From Their Own Mistakes

Even when you are right it's not always helpful to insist on your point of view. Parents know that sometimes they have to be Parakeets when dealing with their children.

When Susan was seventeen she inherited some money from her grandmother's estate. She quickly determined what she wanted to do with the unexpected windfall – she was going to buy a car. Her parents, however, were of the opinion that her money was best saved and used when she went off to college the next year. They knew that expenses were going to add up and she would be fortunate to have this extra financial buffer. They argued about it. Susan's parents reminded her that it wasn't just the purchase of a car but the maintenance that would cost her. She reminded them that she was old enough to make her own decisions. No matter what they said, Susan insisted that it was her money and she should be allowed to spend it the way she wanted. The conflict was putting a definite strain on their relationship.

Finally, Susan's parents decided that the only way Susan was going to understand the expenses that come with owning a car was if she actually experienced it. They knew they wouldn't always be able to help her in making her financial choices. They agreed that she should decide what she wanted to do with the money. They gave in so that Susan could learn from her own mistakes.

You Don't Have To Be A Parakeet All The Time

If you find yourself behaving as a Parakeet in most conflict situations you probably have difficulty imagining dealing with conflict in any other way. Certainly there are those situations when being a Parakeet has been the best approach. But if you find yourself taking a Parakeet approach too often, here are some things you might want to consider in order to change your behavior.

Focus On The Problem

Don't make it personal. Just because you disagree with someone about something doesn't mean they're not a good person. The same goes for you. Conflict does not define your relationship. In fact, it is a part of all healthy relationships.

When you find yourself in a conflict situation, focus on the problem rather than the person you have the conflict with. Instead of concerning yourself with how that other person might view you or the negative effects of the conflict, think about the issue itself and some possible options for resolution.

Speak Up

State your own concerns. Clearly define your perspective. Tell the other party what you think. As difficult as it may seem, articulate your views on the matter.

When possible, be first to state your position. If you wait to hear what the other party wants and simply respond to them you will likely find yourself agreeing with them without stating your position. Think about what you want or need and speak up.

Don't Assume

It is important that you don't make assumptions about what the other party may need or want. Don't even assume that there will be a conflict. When you anticipate the other party's position, you are dealing with imaginary conflict rather than the real thing. If you think the other person sees things differently than you do, you won't know until they tell you. So ask. You may be surprised by the response.

Remember That It's Not A Popularity Contest

You will find yourself in situations where asserting yourself will jeopardize the relationship. But there are times when it's just not important that you're well liked or that a relationship remains intact. Sometimes the issue is so important that you need to make the unpopular decision. Sometimes you need to insist on your way even if that means the other party will be angry with you. Sometimes preserving that relationship simply isn't as important as the issue at hand. But choose your battles wisely. Consider the long-term consequences. Are you likely to be dealing with this issue again if you give in now? If so, then you may need to be more assertive.

Acknowledge The Relationship

You place a great value on the relationship so admit it. But remember, a relationship without conflict is not a real relationship. That's not to say you have to have a big blow up regularly to be healthy, but occasional differences of opinion are normal. Using Parakeet behavior and glossing over your differences or agreeing just to make the conflict go away can actually destroy a relationship rather than enhance it. If you want to preserve the relationship, be willing to engage in conflict from time to time.

Tips For Dealing With Parakeets

When you are in conflict with Parakeets it is important that you provide them with an environment that is non-threatening. When Parakeets feel safe and secure they will find it easier to express their point of view.

Communicate

Communication is vital to dealing with a Parakeet. Listen to what the Parakeet says but also to what the Parakeet doesn't say. "I can live with that" does not connote enthusiasm for what you're suggesting. Parakeets may not be quick to articulate their position. You will need to ask and be patient. If Parakeets are reassured that the relationship is not threatened and that you do want to know what they think, they are more likely to enter into dialogue with you.

Acknowledge Feelings

The Parakeet may express feelings that don't seem logical to you. "I feel horrible when we argue" may not make sense to you because it's not how you feel. But ignoring or dismissing the Parakeet's feelings is hurtful to the Parakeet. These feelings are a significant part of how the Parakeet views the conflict. Acknowledging these feelings as real, whether or not they make sense to you, is key to finding a solution that works for both of you.

Don't Offer Solutions Too Quickly

When dealing with Parakeets, it is important that you refrain from offering solutions too quickly. Parakeets are anxious to find out what you want and quick to agree so that the conflict can be put to rest. It is important that you take every opportunity you can to explore the issue and see both sides of the issue before determining what might be an appropriate solution.

Be Realistic

Some people are their own worst enemies. It seems as if they get themselves boxed into a corner. Parakeets may make unrealistic commitments to you when you are in conflict because they want to smooth it over and put those negative thoughts and feelings behind them. It's easy to say, "Well, if that's what they're willing to agree to, they're going to have to figure out how to make it work," even when we know it's unrealistic. We know they're going to have difficulty living up to that commitment yet we don't challenge it because it's what we wanted. But remember, if the Parakeet can't live up to his commitment then you're not getting what you wanted anyway. You might as well acknowledge it and see if you are able to come up with a more realistic solution.

Let Them Know They're Valued

Remember that Parakeets need to know that they are valued and that your relationship with them is important to you. It will be important to reassure them of this from time to time, even in the middle of a conflict.

Parenting experts tell us that we must make a distinction between disapproving of a behavior and disapproving of a child. It's the same thing with Parakeets. Make sure that they are aware that you are making a distinction between the issue at hand and them as a person.

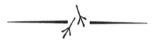

5

Owls

Victor The Owl

Victor was the president of a small software development company that began with a dozen employees. Within a year, they had increased to just over one hundred staff. In their time of quick growth, Victor was aware of increased frustration and discontent amongst some of his staff. He knew that as long as employees were unhappy or had any negative feelings toward their colleagues, they would not be working at their best. He knew he needed to do something about the low morale.

Victor brought his management team together and was very upfront with them. "We seem to have a problem. There is a sense of negativity that is developing and permeating our work environment. We need to know where this negativity has come from and how it has affected our team. We need everyone to be pulling in the same direction and this can't happen if everyone is not enthusiastic about where we're headed and what we're trying to accomplish. What are the issues affecting our staff? How can we address them? We need to establish and maintain a positive and productive work environment. Let's talk about this and see what ideas we can come up with."

The group was silent for a moment and then Gary, one of the managers who had been with the company from the beginning, spoke up. "We've grown so quickly that I don't think we've had time to adequately develop our corporate structure. There is confusion about who is responsible for what and who is accountable to whom. Those of us who have been with this company since the beginning know what we're trying to accomplish and are really committed to the success of this company. We all know that you've got to jump in wherever you're needed to get the job done. But some of our new employees look at this as just a job and wait at their stations until someone tells them what to do. They're lazy and not proactive and they're pulling us down."

With that, several others at the table gave their perspective on the situation. Many of them agreed with Gary's assessment, citing other examples and adding to his explanation. Victor listened to what these managers had to say, responding and asking questions as they continued to discuss the situation. The meeting went on for several hours. At one point Victor noticed that Francine, who was relatively new to the company, had not contributed to the discussion. He called upon her. "Francine, we haven't heard from you. It would be valuable for us to understand, as someone who has joined us quite recently, if your assessment of the situation coincides with what is being said here."

"Frankly, I see it differently," she stated. "I think you need to understand that most of us who have joined the company in the past few months came here after having been laid off elsewhere. We are people with experience in this field. We also have experience with the volatility of the high tech sector. We know that jobs come and go. Why should we believe this company is any different?"

At the adjournment of the meeting, Victor thanked everyone for his or her contributions to the discussion. They did not conclude with consensus about the cause or the solution to the negative attitudes in the workplace.

Several days later, Victor knocked on Francine's office door. "Do you have a few minutes? I'd really like to explore what you said the other day at our meeting a little further." And for the next hour they discussed Francine's experiences and her perspective on the current work environment.

The following day, at another manager's meeting, Victor suggested that they enlist the help of a consultant. "We would benefit by the expertise and perspective of someone who is outside the organization so that we can more fully understand the dynamics at play and develop a more positive work environment." Everyone agreed and a consultant was brought in to analyze the company's work environment.

When the consultant reported her initial findings, Victor had numerous questions. He ended the meeting by saying, "What you're discovering here is fascinating and enormously beneficial for us. It is an incredibly complex issue." Victor asked the consultant to explore further so they could better understand the challenges the company faced. This happened several times. Each time the consultant would report to Victor he would ask the consultant to explore further so that they could have a more complete picture of the situation. Several times Victor suggested that the consultant go back and interview staff members that she had already interviewed. "I know that you've already spoken to them. But they have a very unique perspective and I don't think that the initial hour you spent with them allowed them to really share their insights with you."

This went on for several months. Each week, at the managers' meeting, Victor would update the managers on the ongoing workplace assessment and the work of the consultant, saying that the issues required further exploration. Many of the managers were growing increasingly frustrated by the continuous exploration without any definitive answers or plans of action. Finally one of the managers, Michelle, had to speak up. "This has gone on too long. We don't need to do any further study of why there is negativity in our workplace. I think we have demonstrated why right here. It's because nothing ever gets decided or gets done. We talk and talk and talk but we never take action. We've spent countless hours of our time and staff time and a lot of money on a consultant but all we've done is talk about the problems we have. We haven't found any solutions. We haven't done anything. I wasn't negative about this whole process to begin with but I sure am now!"

Victor was an Owl. He knew they had a problem with negativity amongst the staff and wanted to fully explore what was happening and why. And it seemed there were always more questions to be asked and more issues to understand. All of this took a great deal of time and effort. And Victor was willing to invest the time and effort. But many of the other staff found this frustrating. They saw it as procrastination and spinning their wheels. They weren't getting anywhere. Even when Michelle voiced her frustration, Victor's instinctual response was to ask her more questions about why she felt the way she did. This only heightened Michelle's irritation and she walked away from Victor's questions in anger.

The Owl's Characteristics

We say that some people manage conflict like Owls because their behaviors in conflict situations are similar to some of the unique characteristics of owls.

Aware

Owls are birds that can see all around them. They have very flexible necks so that they can rotate their heads two hundred and seventy degrees around. This means that they can see what is happening on all sides of them. There is very little that happens around an owl that the bird is not aware of.

Those who manage conflict like Owls also want to be aware of everything that is going on around them. Owls want to look at the situation from every angle. They need to understand where the conflict came from and why. They also pride themselves in anticipating conflict and recognizing it before those around them recognize it. Owls clearly have their own point of view or perspective on the conflict but they want to be able to see it from the other person's point of view as well.

Perceptive

Owls have long been the symbol for wisdom. It may be because of how they appear as they perch on a branch and survey the activity around them. It may also be because owls are known for their excellent hearing as well as sight. They can see well at night and have what is called *binocular vision* which allows owls to judge the distances between objects. They can see detail at great distances. Their hearing is so acute that they can detect exactly where a sound is coming from. They can also hear very quiet sounds.

In conflict, Owls hear things that other people may miss. When an Owl experiences conflict he will look for meaning and significance in each word that is spoken and every action that is taken. The Owl will not be content to deal only with the obvious issues. The Owl will want to delve into the underlying issue or issues. The Owl will constantly be asking why: Why has this happened? Why is the other party seeing it differently? Why is it important? Why are they not able to reach agreement?

Slow moving

Owls will sit practically motionless for hours. They will perch and watch what is happening around them but with the minimum of movement. When they do finally move, their movement is slow. While many birds the size of owls are known for their rapid flight, owls fly quite slowly. Their slow flight does not hinder owls from achieving their goal and capturing their prey, however. Because of the accuracy of their sight and hearing, even flying slowly, owls are exacting hunters.

Those who manage conflict like an Owl are also slow-moving. They take their time to work through conflict situations. Owls are not looking for a quick fix to the problem. They want to make sure they have addressed every issue and every concern to the full satisfaction of all parties involved. This can take considerable time. The Owl is quite willing to discuss the situation at length and repeatedly if necessary.

Owls work through conflict very calmly. They need to analyze the whole situation before determining appropriate action. Even when a solution to the problem has been reached, the Owl will want to analyze the solution to make sure that it is the best possible way to resolve the problem.

Communicative

Owl calls are a significant part of folklore and legend. This is because owls have such a wide range of calls. They hoot, screech, scream, snort, hiss and even purr. Some of their sounds are quite eerie while others are remarkably human-like. When a group of owls vocalizes together the sound is loud and quite remarkable. In addition to their vocal communication skills, owls have very expressive body language. Owl observers can tell a great deal about the owls by their posture, the way they are holding their head, and the state of their feathers.

Those who adopt an Owl conflict management style are also very vocal. Communication is vital to an Owl. Everything about the conflict must be talked through. Owls are usually quite skilled at communicating with others, even in stressful situations such as conflict. They are able to explain their perspective, usually in significant detail. They will ask a great number of questions in order to understand the other party's position as well. Owls will usually want to talk to the other party about the conflict on more than one occasion. They do so in order to make sure that the solution to the conflict is a long term one.

The Owl's Tactics

The Owl is most concerned with finding a resolution to the conflict that addresses the interests of all parties involved. The Owl wants to fully understand all perspectives in order to do so.

Owls are not generally hesitant to get involved in conflict. In fact, others who experience conflict with Owls report that Owls frequently *make a mountain out of a molehill.* While the other party does not see the issue as significant, the Owl wants to delve in and discuss it beyond what the situation warrants.

Here are a few typical Owl tactics.

Questions

Owls are information gatherers. They will ask questions constantly – of themselves and the other party. They are willing to do a great deal of self-exploration. They want to understand themselves and their own motivation so that they can explain it to the other party. They want to understand the other person's position. They want to know everything that happened that led to the conflict.

Frank's teenage daughter wanted to go on a weekend camping trip with a group of friends. Frank didn't want his daughter to go – he thought she was too young and didn't feel that he knew the group of young people well enough to trust them.

As an Owl, Frank approached the conflict with a series of conversations over several days. One of their exchanges went something like this.

"I'm not convinced that you kids can handle camping on your own. Does anyone have camping experience?"

"Some of them have been camping before. They know what they're doing."

"But you've never been that interested in camping. Why now?"

"I just want to go and have a good time with my friends."

"So it's not really the camping experience that's so important? If they were doing something else you'd want to do that instead?"

"Yeah."

"So are there other things that you could do that would be safer for all of you?

"Dad, they want to go camping."

"How well do you know these kids you want to go with? This isn't your usual crowd is it?"

"They're a good group of kids, Dad."

"Who are they? Have any of them been over here?"

He could have just said no – a Woodpecker father probably would have! But Frank and his daughter had numerous discussions about the situation and every time, Frank asked questions. He wanted to completely understand what his daughter wanted and why she wanted it.

Analysis

As Owls gather information they will analyze everything they hear and see. They want to understand what everything means. They are not content to deal with issues only at a surface level and will be easily frustrated by others who try to do so. Owls will usually see the actual confrontation between two parties as simply a symptom of a much larger and more complex issue.

We were called in to an organization to work with two company vice presidents who were experiencing conflict. When the situation was described to us, it seemed that the issues were quite straightforward and probably could be dealt with fairly quickly if both parties were willing. The two individuals involved expressed their desire to work through their differences and were appreciative of any assistance they could get. We thought that a single session together would be sufficient. Unfortunately, we had not bargained for the fact that both parties in the conflict were Owls. After several hours of talking through the conflict and what had happened, one party announced that "Really, this situation is only the tip of the iceberg. There are much larger issues at play here."

One session was not going to be enough time for these two Owls to work through the conflict. Several sessions later they were both making comments like "Last time when we were discussing this situation I wasn't sure that you were able to adequately express your concerns." And "It seems to me that we need to talk about this part of the problem a little more." And "I think we need to delve a little deeper here."

Although the two parties were quickly on good terms with each other, they wanted to spend considerable time analyzing why this conflict had unfolded as it had, what factors were at play in the workplace that could result in other staff experiencing the same sort of conflict, and how their solution could be integrated into the everyday workings of their organization.

Talk, Talk, Talk

Owls never seem to tire of talking and processing the issues at play in relationships. This is because they want to find a solution that will address all the needs of all parties involved. They will frequently use the language of *us* rather than *you* or *I* because they see conflict as an opportunity to engage in dialogue together. The focus is on what can be discovered and learned together.

Sara told us about her experience living with a family of Owls. Anything that involved any member of the family, she said, seemed to affect everyone. Anyone's problem, whether it involved another family member or someone outside the family, was an important topic of conversation for the entire family. If there was a conflict of any sort, a family meeting was called. Sara reported that these family meetings seemed to go on endlessly. Everyone was expected to share their perspective on the situation, air all of their feelings, and contribute to the solution. If she or her siblings did not actively participate in the conversation, one or other of Sara's parents would be sure to ask "What's your opinion on this?"

Sara also reported that all the Owls in her family walked away from these discussions deeply satisfied. They saw these discussions as an opportunity to work through conflict, see the situation from all angles, and come to the best possible solution. Unfortunately, Sara was not an Owl like the other members of her family. All that Sara could think about was how long and painful those meetings were!

The Owl's Motivation

Owls' behavior in conflict situations is motivated by their basic personal needs. Owls are usually very aware of their needs and are able to articulate exactly what they want in a conflict situation. Owls are usually quite skilled at encouraging others to cooperate with their way of dealing with conflict.

Process

For Owls, the process of working through conflict is the driving force or motivation behind their behavior. They need to deal with the conflict intentionally and thoroughly. Their need is the process itself. In working through the conflict in this way, the Owl attempts to come to the best possible solution – one that is correct and harmonious. But it is not the solution alone that is important to Owls; it is the method by which that solution has been reached.

We hear more and more about new ways to deal with conflict that are non-adversarial. Processes like mediation, conciliation, and negotiation require both parties to become involved in discussing their differences and working towards a solution together. These processes are not overly complex but can be vital to working through conflict constructively. They are the kind of processes that Owls feel quite comfortable with and are quite willing to get involved in.

When Owls find themselves in a conflict situation and the other party is willing to talk about the conflict, Owls usually gets some degree of satisfaction. They may not have their needs fully met if the other party is not willing to engage the process in the in-depth way the Owl is, however. The Owl's need for process can be further broken down into two distinct aspects: personal growth and dialogue.

Personal growth

Owls value their own ideas and perspectives. Owls will not hesitate to state their opinions. They are quite willing to share their views and don't try to make them more palatable or less confrontational. But this does not mean that Owls will stubbornly adhere to their positions no matter what.

Because Owls are so aware of their own positions in the conflict, they are open to listening to the ideas and opinions of someone else. In fact, Owls want to know and understand the other person's point of view. Owls are interested in the other's perspective because Owls look for ways to address the other person's needs as well as their own.

Owls need to feel that they are learning something and growing through the conflict process. Owls want to deal with others with integrity – they want to do the right thing and they want to build the relationship, making it stronger. Owls want to come out of the conflict knowing that the parties involved have dealt with it in the best possible way so that everyone involved in the conflict has learned from their experience and the conflict is not likely to recur.

Dialogue

The communication process in dealing with conflict is actually something that Owls need. Owls want to know that there is dialogue, that no one is contributing more or less than the other person, and that there is an exchange or an integration of ideas. For Owls, good decisions only come by talking them over with others – in their opinion, this allows for creativity. In communicating with others, Owls are seeking out ideas and perspectives that are different than their own.

Because Owls need dialogue, they like to follow a process for dealing with conflict. They need to know that issues have been itemized, that each issue has been adequately discussed and that the parties have had the opportunity to express themselves freely and fully.

Dialogue is so much a part of the Owl's needs that, even when a solution to a conflict can easily be reached, the Owl will want to discuss further what happened, how it happened, and why it happened. The Owl will want to explore the resolution, making sure the conflict won't happen again. Those who come into conflict with Owls often complain that the Owl just "won't let it go" or that they want to "talk the situation to death."

What To Expect When You're An Owl

Many people who use the Owl conflict management style find that they are able to resolve conflicts in a positive way and get results that all involved parties are happy with. This is certainly the case when this style is used appropriately. There are those situations, however, in which the Owl conflict management style is not the most appropriate. Using the Owl conflict management style in every conflict situation can have negative effects for both the Owl and the other party.

Superiority

Owls are usually pretty self-confident about the approach they take to conflict. Owls want to engage the other party and work through their differences. Owls are willing to listen to the other party's perspective. It all sounds so reasonable. The Owl can't help but wonder why anyone would not be willing to work through conflict in this way.

When an Owl comes into conflict with someone who is utilizing a different conflict management style, the Owl will work to coax that other party into cooperating and adopting the Owl approach. The Owl will say things like "If we just talk this out, I know we can find a solution," or "If we both put our heads together I know we can find our way out of this."

If the other party does not want to adopt the Owl conflict management style, the Owl will get very frustrated with the other party's lack of cooperation. There is a sense of insult that the other party will not accept the Owl's invitation to approach conflict in such a productive way. Owls consider themselves to have been reasonable and the other party as unreasonable. It becomes easy, then, for the Owl to have a sense of superiority in the situation thinking, "I was willing to work through this thoughtfully and productively. He's the one who refused."

Manipulation

In dealing with an Owl, some people will report a sense of being swept away by the Owl and feeling that they were given no choice but to become involved in a rather lengthy and involved process. "I just wanted him to be a little more tidy around the house and he wants to talk about the meaning of life!" was the reaction of one Owl's spouse.

Because the Owl wants to delve into every possible aspect of the conflict, the Owl frequently sees a particular situation as part of a much larger whole. So, in order to resolve the situation, the Owl wants to engage the other party in a discussion about the larger issues. For the other party, this may result in a feeling of being manipulated. It may appear that the Owl is trying to distract the other party from the issue at hand.

Because the Owl conflict management style relies on communication to such an extent, experienced Owls generally have good communication skills. They are experienced in articulating their thoughts and emotions, their values and their issues. Many people who come into contact with Owls may feel intimidated or controlled by the Owl's verbal skills. They feel that they have to keep up with the Owl in terms of contributing to the dialogue yet don't always know how to articulate their perspective in the same skilled way that the Owl does. It may seem as if their point of view is not as valid as the Owl's because it has not been expressed as clearly.

The Owl conflict management style requires time, patience and introspection. But there are those who do not want or need the level of self-awareness and personal growth when dealing with conflict that the Owl strives for. Many people experience extreme frustration with the Owl's time-consuming need to explore and understand the meaning of every word and action. They feel that the Owl is simply asking too much of them when the Owl expects them to become involved in this process. The other party may feel that the Owl is simply procrastinating or hoping to get the upper hand by frustrating the other party. The other party feels exasperated and may refuse to participate in any further discussion.

Two Winners

Generally speaking, when the Owl conflict management style is used there is a sense of a satisfactory outcome for both parties. It is a true win – win situation. Both parties will have invested a great deal of time in discussion and exploration of the situation, of their relationship, and of possible solutions. Because of the time invested in the process and because of the depth to which the situation is explored, both parties will have made a significant investment in arriving at the resolution and agreeing that it was the right thing to do.

Because of the depth to which Owls explore conflict, the result is generally a new intensity to the relationship. The two conflicting parties have experienced something significant together. They likely have learned something about themselves and the other person. They understand each other to a greater degree. Conflict for Owls is a bonding experience. While the conflict may not result in friendship, it does result in a deeper relationship.

When To Be An Owl

There are a number of situations in which the Owl conflict management style is the best choice. Because the Owl style is a very coopera-

tive one, you will frequently hear that it is always the best way to deal with conflict. But this is not the case. There are appropriate uses for all conflict management styles. When considering whether or not the Owl style is the best one to use, the important question to ask is whether the outcome of the conflict is important enough for the investment of time and energy that you will have to give. There are those situations where you can honestly say it's just not worth it. Here are some situations where it would be appropriate to use the Owl conflict management style.

When You Need New Ideas

We said earlier that conflict can have positive results. One of those positive results can be to learn something new. In fact, some of the best and most creative new ideas have been a result of conflict.

Owls do not come into a conflict situation with a predetermined idea of what the solution to the conflict is. Woodpeckers do – they want the solution to be their solution. Parakeets do as well – they want the solution to be the other party's solution. But Owls want to come up with an integrated, cooperative solution. This means that the process of working through a conflict like an Owl can be an extremely creative one. The Owl is willing to take ideas from all parties concerned and integrate them into a new, previously unconsidered solution. Using the Owl conflict management style is a learning experience. It is an opportunity to think outside the box and discover new ideas.

When the old way of doing things hasn't worked and a new way of doing things is necessary, taking the Owl approach is most appropriate.

When Conflicts Are Long-Standing

Many relationships break down over time. Rarely is overwhelming conflict the direct result of a single event. More frequently, there is a *straw that breaks the camel's back,* so to speak. When conflicts have built up over a significant period of time it is important to take the time to work through the feelings and events that are a part of conflict.

The longer it has taken for a conflict to develop, the longer it will take to resolve. There are more deep-seated issues, buried feelings, and events that need to be talked about and explored. The whole pattern of how the conflict developed needs to be understood in order for it to be resolved. In situations such as this, the Owl conflict management style is appropriate.

When You Need A Long-Lasting Solution

Have you ever experienced those conflicts that just keep coming back again and again? Sometimes we have a problem and come up with a short-term solution; something that will solve things for the moment but we know that we're going to be faced with it again later. That's okay for some conflict situations. When you want to go out to an Italian restaurant for dinner and your spouse prefers a Chinese restaurant, a quick compromise will work for the moment. Likely you will run into other occasions when you and your spouse disagree about where you want to go for dinner but the thought of being faced with that conflict again is not overwhelming.

But there are other conflicts that we really don't want to have to revisit. We would like them resolved once and for all. With the Owl approach to conflict this is possible. Owls consider it essential to be in dialogue with others when resolving conflict. The Owl respects the ideas and feelings of the other party and looks to incorporate those into any resolution. The Owl also expects the other party to participate in finding solutions and to be a significant part of making any solution work. Because of this respect for the other party, there is participation from all sides when a solution is reached. Because all parties have personally invested in the solution, the commitment to making the solution work is long lasting.

You Don't Have To Be An Owl All The Time

If you are an Owl, it may surprise you to know that not everyone shares your enthusiasm for working through conflict. You may find it difficult to understand that the Owl approach is not always the best approach to conflict. But, if you use the Owl approach exclusively, you run the risk of alienating the other party and not resolving the issue at all. Here are a few things to consider.

Remember That Not Everyone Is Like You

Not everyone shares your sense of fairness and need for long-lasting resolution. You cannot force someone into greater self-awareness. What you perceive to be a very reasonable approach is not necessarily the most reasonable approach to the other party. If the other party does not see the importance of dialogue on the issue then they will not engage in a lengthy discussion. It takes two people to have a conversation.

Be Quiet

There is an ancient Chinese proverb that says, *When the student is ready, the teacher will appear.* You can talk and talk and talk to someone all you want, but if they are not ready or willing to listen, there is no communication. When you find yourself in a conflict situation, the other party may not be ready to engage in a process of working through that conflict. You can talk and explain and analyze all you want, but it doesn't change the fact that they are not ready. There is great power in silence. Wait. When the other person is ready to explore and examine your differences, they will tell you.

Read Reactions

Learning to read your audience is an invaluable skill. In your earnestness to talk through everything you may lose the other party. It is important to know when they have withdrawn or disengaged. Recognize that your behaviors don't always have the desired effect and that it's not always the other party's fault! The other party may believe that you are avoiding the main issue or trying to manipulate the situation. Although they may not state it in words, the other party may be asking you to back off. Make sure that you are watching for signals from the other party that let you know they are willing to proceed.

Focus On The Solution

It is tempting for Owls to get mired in the history and intricacy of a conflict. Conflict can be very complicated, but if we spend too much time analyzing why the conflict happened in the first place, we will never get to a solution. If you are an Owl, keep focused on the solution by asking, "how can we fix this?" rather than "how did we end up with such a mess?"

Prioritize

Not all aspects of the conflict are equally important. Therefore, not everything requires the same amount of examination and discussion. Prioritize by determining which issues need time and attention and which ones don't. But be aware that your priorities and the other person's priorities may not be the same. Don't assume that you know what the other person thinks. Ask them what is most important to them.

Tips For Dealing With Owls

When you find yourself in conflict with an Owl, the Owl will assume that you are willing to engage in dialogue and a process to work through your differences. Owls are quite willing to direct the process, itemizing issues, determining when issues require further discussion and exploration, and asking questions. In order to deal with Owls and not feel manipulated by this process, here are a few things to keep in mind.

Communicate

When dealing with an Owl it is important to keep the lines of communication open. You will need to participate fully in the dialogue – this means talking about your own position but also listening to the Owl's position. Owls will probably be able to convey their position quite clearly. If you do not feel as articulate as the Owl, don't be too quick to verbalize your thoughts. When you feel overpowered or overwhelmed by the Owl's communication style it is okay to ask for time to get your thoughts together. Just make sure you tell the Owl what you need. The Owl needs to know that you are willing to talk things through. The Owl doesn't generally mind how long the process will take as long as you are willing to participate.

Be Honest

You need to let Owls know what you are thinking. When you don't agree, say so – Owls will not be put off by differences. Be willing to talk about your position and be clear about what you need. Tell Owls how you see the situation and what possible solutions would work for you. Be honest and realistic. This type of information will put Owls at ease. It gives them something to work with.

You can be assured that Owls will not disregard your position. Owls are truly interested in your position and will be reasonable. Owls want to know what you are thinking because they want to be able to address your concerns, not because they are trying to find your weakness.

Be Proactive

Be proactive in your discussions with Owls. Don't just wait to respond to what the Owl has to say. Make observations and suggestions. Ask Owls questions about their position and the way that they see things. While this may initially seem time-consuming, it actually moves the process along. If Owls do not feel that you are participating in a process of working through the conflict, they will need to spend more time exploring issues and asking questions. Owls will do this in an effort to engage you. Owls will take the lead and direct the process if they think it is necessary. If you demonstrate that you are actively engaged in the process, the Owl's need for dialogue will be satisfied and the process can continue.

Provide Feedback

Give Owls feedback. Tell Owls what you think about what they are saying. Owls are constantly reading between the lines or looking for the underlying meaning. If you don't provide feedback, Owls are likely to make assumptions and attribute meaning or significance to things. With feedback Owls will know your position and can respond to it rather than getting sidetracked by assumptions.

Chantal told us of her experience as an Owl when getting more feedback would have been helpful. Chantal was a team leader. She was aware that management had made changes to the policy regarding how vacation time was booked. Their company had always had a first come first served attitude toward vacation time but the company had now adopted a rather complex process of rotation and prioritizing based on the employee's position and years of service. Although she was not responsible for the new policy, she was obligated to enforce it with her team of employees. She was concerned that the new process would be frustrating and annoying to her staff. She brought the team together to discuss the issue. When her opening comments were met with silence, she assumed that the employees were so angry that they were unwilling to discuss the issue. She proceeded to explain how the new procedures could work to their benefit. When they still did not respond, Chantal suggested that she would meet with each employee individually to work through their planned vacation time. As the staff members left the meeting, Chantal overheard one employee saying to the other "I know the new policy looks complicated but it really doesn't change anything for us. I don't know why she's making such a big deal out of it." The employees were not upset or concerned about the process at all. But without feedback, Chantal made many assumptions about the significance of the issue. Consequently she spent more time on the problem than the situation warranted.

Set Guidelines

If you find yourself in a conflict situation with an Owl, set reasonable guidelines for the process. Owls are willing to discuss and revisit issues at length. If you do not want to participate in a rather lengthy process, set some parameters around it. This may include timelines, agendas and goals. You might say something like "Let's work through this issue but by the end of our meeting today we need to reach some conclusions," or "What we really need to talk about is what to do about this issue. Let's concentrate on that right now."

By setting these guidelines you are participating in defining the process. You will then have a sense of where the process is going and what is expected of you. You will also have some control over the time invested in the process. And the Owl will be satisfied because the process engages both parties.

6

OSTRICHES

Marvin the Ostrich

Stan was regional head of the sales department for a large manufacturing company. He had recently received notice from head office about a new product line that the company was about to introduce. He had also received his region's sales targets for the coming months. He was concerned. He did not believe that adequate market analysis had been done to determine if the new product would sell. Knowing his region as he did, he knew the new product wasn't going to interest his clients. He didn't see how he could possibly fulfill his targets. Stan's supervisor, Marvin, was director of sales and Stan had talked to him about his misgivings several months ago when they first discussed the potential of a change to the product line. If this notice was any indication, Marvin hadn't heard a word Stan had said.

Stan sent Marvin an e-mail outlining some of his concerns. When he had not received a response in three days, Stan sent another e-mail. He still received no response. Stan knew that Marvin was a busy man but he felt he needed to make Marvin aware of his apprehension about the success of the new product line. Stan also wanted to hear Marvin's perspective. Maybe some market analysis had been done that Stan wasn't aware of. Maybe there were long-range plans that Stan didn't know about that would alleviate some of his concerns.

Stan tried to get Marvin on the phone. Every time Stan called, Marvin's executive assistant answered. She was a terrific gatekeeper. She kept telling Stan how busy Marvin was and that she was sure he would get back to Stan at his earliest convenience. When two weeks went by and Marvin had not returned any of Stan's seven phone calls, Stan knew he wasn't going to get through to Marvin.

Several weeks later Stan was working late tabulating sales figures for his region. Once again he was faced with evidence that this new product line was not selling the way head office was expecting. Stan believed that there was still an opportunity to do some damage control but he needed to speak to Marvin. He decided to call Marvin's office. He would leave a strongly worded message and maybe he would get a response.

Unexpectedly, Marvin answered his phone. He too was working late and his executive assistant had already gone home. Here was Stan's chance to get his message across to Marvin.

"Marvin, I'm glad I got you. I've been trying for weeks. I've got some concerns about this new product line and we need to talk about it."

Stan's comments were met with silence.

"Marvin? Are you there?"

Still no answer.

"Marvin? It's Stan – Eastern Region. Are you there?"

"How did you know I'd be here?"

"I didn't but I'm sitting here looking at sales projections and we've got a potential disaster on our hands. This new product line is not going to give us the results you're anticipating."

"I'm sure everything's going to turn out fine, Stan. Say, did you hear that Charles and his wife went to the Bahamas for two weeks? Don't you wish we could all take that kind of time?"

"Marvin, I'm serious. We need to talk. I'd just like to go over some of my thoughts with you. I have some questions but I also have some ideas. I've been talking to the other district heads and they'd really like to be in on that kind of meeting. We could be at head office just as soon as you set the date and time."

"Well, I don't know, Stan. I'm really busy. You know how it is this time of year."

"This is really important, Marvin."

"I don't see how I could possibly find the time until the middle of next month."

"It can't wait that long, Marvin. Come on, this is going to affect the company's bottom line. We need to meet soon."

"Okay, okay. Let me look at my schedule."

Marvin put Stan on hold. When Stan had been waiting for Marvin to return to the phone for over ten minutes, he figured that Marvin was not going to come back on the line. Just as Stan was about to hang up the phone, he heard Marvin pick up.

"Stan?"

"Yeah, I'm still here, Marvin."

"Oh, oh, yeah. So how are you?"

"I'm getting a little frustrated, Marvin. Did you check your schedule? When can we meet?"

"I'm sorry, Stan, what was that? There seems to be a lot of static on the line. I can't hear you very well."

It took Stan another twenty minutes on the phone before Marvin finally agreed on a meeting date and time. As he hung up the phone, Stan wondered whether or not Marvin would actually be at the meeting. He wouldn't be surprised if Marvin's assistant called him and told him that Marvin was not available after all.

Marvin was an Ostrich. He did not want to participate in a confrontation or anything that even smelled of conflict. When Stan tried to let Marvin know there was a conflict, Marvin avoided Stan as best he could.

The Ostrich's Characteristics

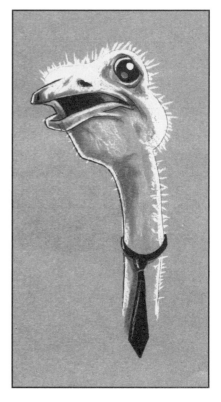

Those who deal with conflict like Marvin are called Ostriches. Many of their characteristics in conflict situations bear a striking resemblance to the bird.

Avoiding

Most people associate ostriches with an image of them burying their heads in the sand when they see danger coming. But ostriches don't actually bury their heads in the sand. It is uncertain where this myth comes from, but it is a fact that ostriches do lie on the ground with their neck outstretched as low to the ground as possible when danger approaches – as if to camouflage themselves and remain undetected.

People who use the Ostrich conflict management style can't bury their heads in the sand, either. But sometimes they'd like to! People who behave as Ostriches in conflict will attempt to avoid the conflict. They will not speak out or draw attention to themselves in any situation that would likely result in conflict. They prefer to *lie low* and hopefully any harsh feelings or ugly confrontations will just pass them by.

It may appear as if Ostriches have not noticed the conflict around them. They likely have noticed but will never admit it. Ostriches attempt to protect themselves by avoiding the situation entirely.

Fast Moving

Ostriches would prefer to remain undetected. But when they are unable to do so, they run. In fact, ostriches are incredibly fast runners, reaching speeds of sixty miles per hour. If an ostrich sees danger approaching and cannot hide in any way, the ostrich will run away as fast as possible. Because of the ostrich's incredible speed, it quickly outdistances any predator.

Those who are Ostriches in conflict situations will run away as well – figuratively or literally! When tensions increase and conflicts erupt you may find Ostriches getting up and walking away. Of course not all Ostriches are able to physically distance themselves. If they can't physically remove themselves from a conflict situation, Ostriches will mentally remove themselves. They are not likely to engage in a heated exchange or even a friendly battle of wills. They will simply disengage. They will not participate. They will not state their views. If at all possible, they will not even acknowledge that the conflict exists.

Powerful Kicker

As you can imagine, ostriches must have incredibly powerful legs to run at such speeds. They also use those strong legs for another defense mechanism. When they can no longer run, and they can't remain undetected, ostriches kick. And their kick is amazingly effective.

In conflict situations, those who use the Ostrich conflict management style can also have a pretty nasty kick. When Ostriches feel backed into a corner and unable to avoid conflict any more, they will come out fighting. Unfortunately, because all of their energy has been put into avoiding the very situation they now find themselves in, Ostriches will not have a well thought out response. The Ostriches' reaction is usually quite volatile, unpleasant and hurtful. Ostriches may not even be aware of how long they have been avoiding the conflict and so, in the end, overreact.

Heat Resistant

Another interesting characteristic of the ostrich is its tolerance for heat. Ostriches are known to withstand temperatures of fifty-six degrees Celsius without undue stress – seemingly unaware of the heat.

They don't appear to adjust their behaviors in any way to accommodate the heat. They simply ignore it and it doesn't seem to affect them in any way.

Those who utilize the Ostrich conflict management style also seem to be heat resistant. When conflict is bubbling all around them they seem to continue on their merry way, not noticing what is happening around them. Those around them may be extremely upset and the Ostrich will ignore these feelings and carry on as if nothing is amiss.

There are those who call Ostriches *Teflon-coated*. It is as if conflict and disagreement never sticks to them. It does not seem to affect them in any way because they refuse to engage in the conflict situation.

The Ostrich's Tactics

There are numerous tactics that Ostriches use to avoid conflict – and avoidance is really the operative word. True Ostriches will do almost anything to avoid confrontation. Here are the three most common tactics that Ostriches use.

Distancing

Ostriches will physically remove themselves from a conflict situation. If someone starts a difficult conversation or confronts another person with a problem the Ostrich will likely leave the room. Ostriches frequently do this even if they are not involved in the conflict themselves. Ostriches dislike conflict so much that even if others get into conflict and they are around, they become uncomfortable and will leave if possible.

Friends told us of a dinner party in their home. Two of their guests started a political debate that got progressively more intense. While these two guests were good friends, their disagreement became quite loud and emotional. Most of the guests were enjoying the debate because they all shared an interest in politics and were making occasional comments to support one or the other's viewpoint. There was one visitor, however, who grew increasingly uncomfortable. Her discomfort was not with the subject matter but with the intensity of the conflict. She did not participate in the discussion. In fact, it did not take long before she excused herself and left the party.

Sometimes physically removing oneself from a situation simply isn't possible. In such situations Ostriches will try to put their heads low to the ground in an attempt to camouflage themselves. They want to blend into the scenery, hoping no one will notice them and ask them to get involved in the conflict. Do you remember what you used to do in school when the teacher asked a question and you didn't know the answer? You didn't want the teacher to call on you and be exposed. You looked down or looked away and avoided eye contact. You will find Ostriches use body language to distance themselves as well. They get very quiet and their body language makes it clear that they do not wish to get involved.

Denying

Ostriches also have verbal tactics for avoiding or deflecting conflict, the primary one being denial. "I don't know what you're talking about" is a very famous Ostrich line. "I don't recall," "I am not aware of that situation," "I had nothing to do with it," or "I don't have a problem – I don't know where you got that idea from," are all Ostrich statements. Ostriches prefer to deny that the conflict exists.

There's a wonderful story that Bill Cosby tells in his comedy routine about how parents confront their children when they're caught doing something that they shouldn't. As he says, upon discovering the child's misbehavior, the parent's first question to the child is "What are you doing?" The parent does this with a certain tone of voice – that sound of incredulity that the child could even have contemplated doing what he's doing. And what does the child always answer? "Nothing." There is complete and utter denial that anything of any significance is happening. Adult Ostriches frequently have a similar response to conflict.

Ostriches use other verbal tactics to deny conflict as well. They may simply not acknowledge that they've heard you when you confront them with an issue. You've heard of selective hearing before. Well, Ostriches select not to hear anything that sounds angry, emotional or confrontational. They may try to change the subject or divert the discussion into something that seems less conflictive.

Delaying

Ostriches will attempt to delay their response in an effort to put off conflict. They may make noncommittal responses such as "we'll see" or "maybe." The other party often takes this kind of response from an Ostrich as agreement.

One of our clients, Mark, told us of a conflict he had with his colleague. Mark and Josie had an assignment to complete and Mark needed a report from Josie. Mark knew that Josie was not enthusiastic about the assignment. Consequently the report that he needed was at the bottom of Josie's list of priorities. As he left the office on a Friday afternoon, Mark said to Josie, "You know that I need that report by Monday at noon, right?" She didn't look up from her computer but merely nodded.

Mark left the office with a sense of assurance that Josie would have the report finished by Monday at noon. But as far as Josie, an Ostrich, was concerned, she had only acknowledged that she knew Mark wanted the report, not that she would get it done. She didn't think she could get the report finished by Monday. But she knew that telling Mark this would lead to an argument. She chose to delay that confrontation.

The Ostrich's Motivation

Ostriches adopt these avoidance behaviors because they are attempting to meet certain personal needs. In the Ostrich's thinking, engaging in conflict endangers these needs. Therefore conflict must be avoided.

Ostriches rarely state their needs in conflict situations. This is, of course, because they do not wish to acknowledge that conflict exists. But, like all conflict management styles, when the Ostrich always avoids conflict, the results are frequently the opposite of what the Ostrich wants or needs.

Control

Ostriches need a sense of control and constraint. This may seem somewhat unusual because, by fleeing a confrontation, the Ostrich gives up all control of the situation. However, for Ostriches, any emotion or viewpoint that is strongly expressed appears to be out of control. The Ostrich sees anger as an emotion that can overwhelm a person. Ostriches are well aware that people say and do things in anger that they would not normally do. For an Ostrich, the only way to maintain a sense of control is to avoid confrontation altogether. So, when the Ostrich sees conflict coming, he heads the other way.

Safety and Security

"I'd rather be safe than sorry" seems to be the Ostrich's motto. Ostriches find conflict extremely uncomfortable. For Ostriches, conflict is so difficult to address because there are so many things that are unknown and uncertain. It is uncertain how the other party will respond to the Ostrich's perspective or needs. It is uncertain how committed the other party is to the Ostrich's position. It is uncertain whether the other person will really understand the Ostrich's thoughts as he tries to articulate them. It is uncertain whether or not the Ostrich will be able to understand the other person's side of things.

There are many risks in conflict – risk of rejection, risk of further conflict, risk of hearing something the Ostrich didn't want to hear, risk of change, risk of things remaining the same. For the Ostrich, these risks seem insurmountable. They cause such great anxiety because what the Ostrich needs most of all is safety and security. The Ostrich tries to minimize risk and maintain a sense of security by simply refusing to engage in conflict.

To Be Correct

Ostriches want to do the right thing. This may not be evident by their behavior but Ostriches want to be correct. Unfortunately, this need to be correct seems to paralyze the Ostrich. When they don't know what the right thing is, they choose to do nothing at all. And, because conflict situations are full of those unknowns we mentioned earlier, it is very difficult to always know what the right thing to do is.

An Ostrich once explained her avoiding behavior this way. "It's just a lot easier not to get involved in something that is controversial. If I state my opinion someone is sure to disagree. Then I'll have to defend myself and I'm likely to hurt that other person along the way. No one wins so why even start? If I don't say anything at all then the other person can't say I'm wrong, can they?"

What To Expect When You're An Ostrich

Unfortunately, avoiding conflict rarely satisfies the needs that Ostriches have. While they want security and to do the right thing, avoiding conflict usually results in more deeply rooted conflict. Because the conflict has not been dealt with quickly, there is opportunity for it to fester. It almost never just goes away like the Ostrich wants it to!

When the conflict grows and festers it becomes increasingly messy and difficult to deal with. Here is a very clear example of the negative conflict cycle continuing on and on. Ostriches avoid dealing with conflict because they find conflict uncomfortable and upsetting. But by avoiding the conflict, Ostriches actually intensify and escalate the conflict. And so the Ostrich becomes even more uncomfortable and upset.

There are several negative results of avoiding conflict like an Ostrich.

Physical Stress Or Pain

Many Ostriches report physical symptoms when conflict erupts. Ostriches will often feel physically ill (nauseous, headache, heart palpitations) when surrounded by conflict. One manager told us of a clerk who was a bystander when two colleagues had a rather heated argument in his office. When the two warring parties stomped away all was silent for a minute and the clerk, shaking and nearly in tears, told the manager that she needed to go home and couldn't possibly work in such a hostile environment.

Lack Of Respect

In our work we frequently deal with managers and executives who are experiencing conflict. And we run across a lot of Ostriches. When we examine their Ostrich behavior, they seem to be consistently surprised by one thing. Their employees interpret their Ostrich behavior as a lack of respect. In other words, staff members will see the supervisor's avoidance and unwillingness to act as a lack of respect for them. As one client explained to us, "If he respected me or my opinion he would talk to me about it. If he valued my contribution to the organization, he would want to work this problem out. He doesn't seem to want to work it out so he must not care whether I stay or leave."

You can imagine that the same would be true with friends or family members. The "I see nothing" attitude is easily interpreted to mean, "I don't care." The implication then is that if you don't care enough to make things right then you must not care very much about the relationship. The feeling of disrespect works both ways. The person in conflict with the Ostrich feels disrespected by the Ostrich. In turn, that person will frequently have little or no respect for the Ostrich.

Loss Of Relationship

Relationships are built on communication – an exchange of ideas, thoughts and experiences. Ostrich behavior puts limitations on communication. When there is no acknowledgement that conflict even exists, people are simply not being honest with each other. This is not the basis for a full and satisfying relationship.

When a friend's mother was diagnosed with terminal cancer the doctor took the family aside and gave them the prognosis – she had approximately 6 months to live. He said that it was their decision whether they wanted to share this information with their mother or not. They knew that she might not be willing to accept the doctor's diagnosis. It wasn't something they wanted to argue with their mother about. So should they tell her or not? Originally the family was not in agreement about this. Some thought it best to avoid the discussion altogether. Others felt they needed to have this conversation with their mother even though it might prove conflictive. As it turned out, however, none of them could sustain the avoidance. As our friend later explained, "Our relationship with our mother was based on mutual respect, love, and open communication. We simply could not continue to be with our mother and not talk about what was happening. To avoid this very difficult issue would be to damage our relationship."

When conflicts are avoided relationships are lost.

Power Imbalance

When one party is an Ostrich, there is never equity of power. It might appear that the avoider is completely powerless in conflict situations. However, this is not necessarily the case. Think about when you've been on the receiving end of the silent treatment. When a person refuses to talk to you, no dialogue is going to happen unless they change their mind and decide to engage in dialogue. In conflict, you cannot move toward any type of resolution unless the Ostrich decides to stop avoiding. The Ostrich can wield incredible amounts of power by decreeing that certain topics are off limits for discussion.

At the same time, there certainly is the possibility that the Ostrich becomes the powerless one in a conflict situation. Remember that the Ostrich is looking for some sense of control. By refusing to participate constructively in dealing with conflict, Ostriches forfeit any opportunity to influence the outcome.

Two Losers

No one wins when conflict is avoided. There is no resolution and so there is no opportunity for a positive outcome. Consequently no creativity or new thinking is brought to bear on the situation. No one has learned anything. Nothing new or better or more productive has come out of the conflict.

There is the rare occasion when avoiding a conflict actually results in the conflict diminishing over time and seeming to just fade away. But even if this does happen, there are no winners. This is not a positive situation. There have been no lessons learned along the way. No one has any better ideas about how to deal with this type of situation if it were to arise again – and without a real solution, it most certainly will.

When To Be An Ostrich

For Ostriches, every conflict seems like a good one to avoid. For those who are not Ostriches it may seem impossible to imagine that there are conflicts that are better left alone. But there are a number of situations in which using the Ostrich conflict management style, even temporarily, can be useful.

When The Issue Is Unimportant

A participant in one of our workshops once said that the criteria he used to decide whether or not to pursue a conflict situation was the answer to three questions: Will this matter fifteen minutes from now? Will this matter next week? Will this matter in a few months? If the answer to each of these questions was no then he knew that the issue was trivial enough to ignore. This allowed him the opportunity to pick his battles and only engage in those conflicts that really mattered.

It is true that not all differences of opinion are worth pursuing. Not every conflict matters. When the issue is insignificant, and ignoring it won't have any lasting negative effects, it's all right to avoid it. But beware. If you have real Ostrich tendencies, it is easy to justify your avoidance. You might be tempted to convince yourself that something doesn't matter when in reality it does.

When Getting Involved Would Cause More Harm Than Good

There are occasions when the issue is not necessarily a trivial one, but getting involved in a conflict has more negative ramifications than positive ones. Sometimes you do need to walk away.

Jack told us about a situation in which he chose to be an Ostrich. He had just started working for a new company and was temporarily assigned to a work project. He knew that he would only be working with this group for about a month and then would be reassigned to another department. On the first day of work, most of his co-workers stopped by his office, one by one, to welcome him to the project team. Very quickly Jack became aware of a conflict between two persons on the team. Each individual that came to speak to him asked Jack, in one way or another, what he thought of the situation. "I felt like I was being asked to pick sides," said Jack. "I knew that if I said anything at all about the situation I would only make matters worse. I decided to act as if I had no idea what they were talking about. I completely avoided the issue." Jack had no need to get involved in this conflict. It really had nothing to do with him and, because of his temporary status, it would have caused more harm than good if he were to get involved.

When Emotions Are Too Strong

There are some conflicts that can be avoided temporarily. This is the case when emotions are too strong or volatile. In this type of situation, being a temporary Ostrich has its benefits. If emotions are high and the argument is intense, it may be appropriate to ignore the situation temporarily and give people time to cool down. Taking a little time can allow both parties to gain some perspective. But remember, this is a temporary measure only.

When The Conflict Gets Sidetracked

Have you ever noticed that when you are arguing with someone the argument often gets sidetracked? Either party may bring up other issues that have been bugging them that really have nothing to do with the main point of contention. Often these side issues take on a life of their own and the argument becomes focused on them rather than the main issue. Or the conflict becomes so enormous and complex that it is overwhelming. In a situation such as this, it can be beneficial to be an Ostrich. Ignore those peripheral issues that are sidetracking the discussion. Act as if you haven't heard them. But it is important to ignore only those issues that are diverting you from the main point of discussion, not all aspects of the conflict.

When It's None Of Your Business

Real Ostriches would never get involved in a conflict that was none of their business. But there are those people who simply love a good fight. They see potential trouble and they just can't wait to help stir the pot. There are times when people become involved in conflicts that they have no business participating in.

A relative told us of an old woman in their neighborhood who loved to gossip. She seemed to watch everyone's comings and goings and was always on the look out for trouble. She heard shouting and then watched her neighbor drive a little too quickly out of his driveway. Since this was not his normal behavior, the woman told others that this was a clear sign of trouble. Obviously this man and his wife had an argument and he left upset! Word spread and friends and relatives started choosing sides and arguing amongst themselves. By the time the man had returned home, the whole neighborhood was in an uproar.

The man and his wife had indeed had an argument that morning. But a little Ostrich behavior here on the part of the neighbor would have been beneficial. Her neighbor's conflict was none of her business. By getting involved the conflict became increasingly complex and involved more people than was necessary, making it more difficult to resolve.

You Don't Have To Be An Ostrich All The Time

If you are an Ostrich, you may be putting a lot of time and energy into avoiding conflict. In fact, you may not even be aware of the toll it has taken on you or on those around you because you have refused to acknowledge the conflict at all. Think carefully about your experiences with conflict. If you are quick to say, "I have no conflicts" your Ostrich behavior may be out of hand. If you are aware of your strong desire to avoid conflict, there are some things you need to think about in order to change your behavior so that you use the Ostrich approach only in the appropriate situations.

Recognize The Message You're Sending

You need to be aware that by avoiding conflict you convey a lack of concern for others, for their needs, and for any positive resolution between you. It's as if you don't care about anything – not about who they are or how things get done.

Consistent Ostrich behavior shows a lack of respect. This is not likely the message you want the other person to receive. Many Ostriches will quickly say, "It's not about the other person, it's about me." Unfortunately, if you do not talk to the other person about the conflict, there is no way they can know or understand this.

Recognize What's Important

You may be avoiding a conflict because you don't think it warrants your attention – it's just not important to you. But be aware that the other party's needs and concerns are not the same as yours. This issue may be of extreme importance to the other party. For that reason alone, the situation requires some time and effort on your part.

Prevent A Larger Conflict

Deal with it now and you won't have to deal with it later. By avoiding conflict you only prolong the agony. It may be an effort to get involved and work through the conflict but remind yourself that by doing so now you will avoid dealing with a more complex and more difficult situation later on. If you need less conflict in your life, deal with it promptly.

Don't Be The Last To Know

If you avoid conflict all the time, those around you will dismiss you. Because you are hesitant to state your opinion, your opinion becomes meaningless. If you are not willing to confront others when you disagree, you will lose credibility.

Ostriches frequently find themselves out of the loop. They are not kept informed because they don't seem to care. While you may appreciate not getting pulled into every conflict, no one wants to be seen as completely ineffective. If you want your thoughts and opinions to matter, you'll have to be more vocal about them. And you will have to express an interest in what is happening around you – even if that means recognizing conflict where it exists.

Get Involved

Behaving like an Ostrich almost never has the desired results. In fact, it most often produces the exact opposite of what you need. When you need control, avoiding conflict allows things to spiral out of control. When you need safety and security, behaving as an Ostrich means that you always run the risk of the conflict exploding in your face. If you need to be right, refusing to act means that you can't possibly be right.

You must get involved if you hope to have the control that you desire. You can only figure out the right thing to do if you discuss the situation. In fact, in order to get any positive results you will need to acknowledge differences and discuss issues.

Tips For Dealing With Ostriches

When you find yourself involved in conflict and the other party is behaving like an Ostrich, there are several things to keep in mind.

Communicate

Even when Ostriches do not reciprocate, it is important that you continue to communicate. Ask questions that require more than a yes or a no for a response. When you ask questions that Ostriches must answer with a more complete statement, Ostriches are not able to avoid the discussion. As long as Ostriches are able to simply respond positively or negatively to you, Ostriches can leave you guessing as to whether they are really agreeing with you or simply acknowledging that you asked a question. Yes or no responses, to Ostriches, are relatively noncommittal. Using open-ended questions requires more information from the Ostrich.

Remember that how you ask these questions will be as important as what questions you ask. If you are confrontational with the Ostrich, the Ostrich will back away. If you demonstrate curiosity and can maintain a nonjudgmental position, the Ostrich will be more likely to communicate with you.

Remove The Sense Of Urgency

Insisting on a response, shouting, using dramatics, getting emotional or in any way conveying a sense of urgency in dealing with a situation will not have the desired result with an Ostrich. Any of these tactics will only confirm to Ostriches that they do not want to get involved. As much as possible, it is important to maintain a relaxed and composed demeanor. Recognize that you will have to take your time in getting a response from an Ostrich. Slow down the pace. Talk as calmly as possible and don't demand an immediate response from the Ostrich.

Avoid Surprises

Do not spring anything unexpected on an Ostrich. Confronting Ostriches when they are not anticipating it will cause them to run in the opposite direction as fast as they can. Let them know in advance that you want to discuss a certain issue. Give them time to prepare themselves.

Many people who frequently come into conflict with Ostriches find this difficult to do. They know that if you give an Ostrich too much advance notice you run the risk of the Ostrich not showing up at the appointed time and place to have an honest discussion. This can and does happen with Ostriches. If you push too hard or become too insistent Ostriches may feel backed into a corner. And when Ostriches feel trapped they will respond. But the response is usually nasty, hurtful and not well thought through.

It may take some very gentle prodding as well as some patience on your part to engage the Ostrich in dialogue.

Don't Embarrass Them

Embarrassment to Ostriches can mean several things. Catching them unaware or criticizing them publicly can be humiliating to Ostriches. If you insist on confronting Ostriches in this way you will get very little cooperation from them. Once again, a slower pace to your discussion will allow Ostriches to gain more control of their emotions. And it might be best to choose the location of your discussion wisely. Pick a quiet environment where you are both on equal footing.

Remember that Ostriches need a sense of safety and security and that almost any conflict situation jeopardizes that for them. The safer you make the Ostrich feel, the more likely the Ostrich will be able to address the conflict.

Use Positive Reinforcement

Reassure the Ostrich throughout the process. Statements such as "I'm glad we're talking about this," or "I appreciate knowing what you're thinking," or "Now I think I understand where you're coming from," can be encouraging to the Ostrich. Remember that one of the Ostrich's key needs is to feel safe and secure. Reassuring Ostriches allows them to feel safe in dealing with the conflict.

Positive reinforcement when discussing conflictive issues does not assume agreement. You can vehemently disagree with someone and still understand his or her perspective. This is something an Ostrich may not immediately understand but will appreciate when you articulate it.

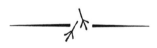

7

HUMMINGBIRDS

Diana The Hummingbird

Diana was the CEO of an international consulting firm. The pace of the work was grueling. Client demands meant hectic schedules and quick turn around time for projects. It always seemed to Diana that there was too much to do and not enough time to do it in. But Diana had to admit that she loved the work and even enjoyed the frenetic pace. If things slowed down she wouldn't know what to do with herself, she always said.

Diana received a call from Jessica, one of her regional managers. Jessica wanted to talk to Diana about a client that they had been dealing with in her region.

"I just want you to be aware of what we've been dealing with here, Diana, and what we've decided to do about it. " Jessica said. She continued by telling Diana about their client, HRA Manufacturing. This client had signed a contract for their consulting services and yet it seemed they were constantly putting roadblocks in the way of getting any actual work done.

"We would set meeting times and they would forget to show up or send someone who had no decision-making authority. And whenever we set targets and deadlines they seemed to ignore them. We'd point out the urgency on something and they'd come up with a reason why it needed to be delayed. I've never seen anything like it in my life."

"Try talking to the company president." asked Diana. "He'll get to the bottom of it."

"We've tried everything, Diana. We've talked, we've sent memos, reminders and e-mails. Nothing seemed to get much of a reaction from them. Except of course, once we sent the invoice. They took notice of that. They're refusing to pay for the time we've put in waiting for them. They don't think they should have to pay for meetings missed because they didn't show up, or extra time we had to put in because of their delays."

"Maybe we can approach this differently. Tell them we can rework the numbers on the current invoice if they commit to completing the project."

"You don't seem to understand, Diana. We've decided to walk away from this one. We've spent a lot of valuable time trying to work with HRA Manufacturing. I don't know why they would sign a contract and then not want the work done but we're not willing to play this game anymore. We just wanted to let you know."

Diana was disturbed by Jessica's willingness to simply put an end to their work with HRA Manufacturing. She realized that it was taking valuable time from other work but she thought there had to be another option.

"How about if we offer them some options on timelines for getting the work done?" suggested Diana. "Perhaps they're not happy with the current timeline. Or we could suggest a scaled-down version of the project. They may be intimidated by the scope of the project. I'm willing to re-negotiate fees as long as we come to an agreement about a schedule."

"Diana, I wasn't looking for solutions or options here. We've decided what we want to do. I am just informing you of our decision."

"But Jessica, I know this isn't a huge project and I know we've got other work to do but I really don't want to burn any bridges here. We said we wanted to get into the manufacturing sector and HRA was our opportunity to build up our expertise. We can't just walk away from that."

"Diana, how can I make this any more clear to you? We've had enough of trying to negotiate with HRA Manufacturing. We don't want to have any more to do with them. I've never said that about a client before but I really don't think this is going to reflect negatively on our company's reputation."

"Okay, okay, I understand your frustration, Jessica. How about if I give the head of HRA Manufacturing a call? Maybe if I have a chat with him we could work things out. Or we could send Pam from central division out to you for a while to cover this project if you've had enough. Sometimes a fresh face and a new voice can get things moving again."

"I really think we need to take a firm stand here, Diana, and I would appreciate you backing my decision."

"But maybe there's another way out of this mess."

Diana continued to look for other options in dealing with their client. And, as Jessica's frustration increased, Diana started looking for options in dealing with her as well.

Diana was a Hummingbird. The thought of taking a firm position in a dispute and refusing to be negotiable was completely foreign to her. As far as Diana was concerned, everything is negotiable and there is always a way to find a solution that works, more or less, for both parties. She was sure they could find something that HRA Manufacturing would agree to and that their consulting firm could live with. And when Jessica was adamant about not wanting to work with HRA Manufacturing any further, Diana continued to look for options that could incorporate her concerns as well.

Jessica's frustration intensified the more Diana generated options. She had called Diana to give her information, not to seek her help in solving a problem. Jessica had not wanted more ideas about why the problem existed or more options on how to fix it. She wanted Diana's support in her position. But for Diana the Hummingbird, Jessica's position was too inflexible and final. Diana wanted to look for a solution that would allow the project to continue. She knew that didn't mean that all the problems were solved but so long as they continued to work together they could continue to address issues as they arose.

The Hummingbird's Characteristics

As with all the conflict management styles, Hummingbirds have some unique characteristics that are very much like the birds they're identified with.

Quick

Hummingbirds move quickly. In fact, they fly at speeds of up to sixty miles per hour. And as they fly, they flap their wings approximately fifty times a second. This means that their wings move so fast that they are just a blur to the human eye.

When dealing with conflict, Hummingbirds are not known for their patience. They want to move through conflict very hastily. It often seems as if there is a time pressure for Hummingbirds. They want a quick fix. Hummingbirds have a tendency to cut to the chase with very little discussion. Even when issues seem complex, the Hummingbird will look for a short cut saying something like "well, if we just do this and this, everything else will work out fine."

Frequently, Hummingbirds move so quickly from issue to issue that the other party cannot keep pace with the Hummingbird's thinking. Even as Hummingbirds present one thought or idea, they are already considering another way of looking at things. While the other party is considering the Hummingbird's position, the Hummingbird is busy developing a new position or perspective.

Hovering

Hummingbirds are flying most of the time. Their tiny feet are almost useless for perching on branches. Even if the hummingbird wants to travel a distance of two inches it must fly. Therefore, hummingbirds do not perch near flowers to feed. They hover in front of the flower, continuing to flap their wings. This means that they do not stay in one place for any significant period of time. They may hover near a particular flower briefly but will quickly move to the next.

In conflict situations, Hummingbirds do not hesitate to change positions. The Hummingbird may hover for a brief time saying, "this is how I think this must be done," or "this is the way I see things," but if the situation is not quickly resolved, Hummingbirds will not adhere adamantly to this position. They will move and change positions suggesting another way to look at things or another option they would be willing to consider, in order to move towards resolution. Hummingbirds may do this numerous times during a conflict.

The Hummingbird is not looking for a sense of finality in dealing with a conflict. According to the Hummingbird, no resolution is an absolute. There is always room for continued negotiation. The Hummingbird is likely to say, "that's good enough for now," in order to move on.

The Hummingbird is not willing to spend a great deal of time working through conflict. The Hummingbird will usually address specific issues with short-term solutions so that the conflict can be resolved for the moment. If there are underlying issues in the conflict, the Hummingbird is not concerned with these. There is never a sense of finality for Hummingbirds so they are not concerned if they have to deal with another aspect of the conflict on another occasion. In fact, the Hummingbird usually anticipates that this will happen and looks forward to the next exchange.

Flexible

Although hummingbirds fly very quickly, they are also able to stop mid-air. And hummingbirds are the only birds that can fly right, left, up, down, backwards and even upside down. They are able to change their direction in what appears to be mid-flight. So, just when you think you know which direction the hummingbird will move next, it surprises you and flies off on a completely different path.

Those who deal with conflict like Hummingbirds are equally flexible. They are able to maneuver and change directions at a moment's notice. When in a conflict situation, Hummingbirds want to explore various options for both why the problem has occurred and what the solution might be. For the Hummingbird this is not a long intensive study of the situation as it might be for the Owl. For the Hummingbird this means a constant shifting of positions. You might hear the Hummingbird say something like "to resolve this I would be willing to do this," and if the other party is not immediately agreeable the Hummingbird will quickly add "or I could do it this way."

For those in conflict with a Hummingbird, it frequently seems that the Hummingbird has no final bottom line or ultimate position. It is often difficult to figure out exactly what is important to Hummingbirds because they are so negotiable.

Energetic

Because they move so quickly and spend a great deal of time in flight, hummingbirds expend a great deal of energy. In fact, in order to maintain that level of energy, hummingbirds must consume two and half times their weight in food daily.

Those who adopt the Hummingbird conflict management style also expend a great deal of energy. By constantly generating more options, maintaining their flexibility and always looking for trade offs and exchanges, dealing with conflict can be exhausting. But to Hummingbirds, conflict is an adventure. Hummingbirds enjoy the give and take, the negotiation of a conflict situation. They see it as a puzzle that needs to be figured out. And the quicker they are able to find the solution to the puzzle, the more exhilarated they feel. Hummingbirds are actually energized by conflict.

The Hummingbird's Tactics

For the Hummingbird, conflict is seen as an imbalance. Hummingbirds want to return to a state of equilibrium and do so as quickly as possible. All of the Hummingbird's tactics are aimed at finding a middle ground or a quick compromise that both parties can agree on.

Trade Offs

Hummingbirds need a sense of movement towards the goal of resolving a conflict. In order to move on, Hummingbirds need to be able to reach middle ground between themselves and the other party. The Hummingbird may not be fully satisfied with the solution reached, but will be adequately satisfied. The assumption on the part of the Hummingbird is that if the other party has been met half way, then the other party will be partially satisfied as well. Therefore the Hummingbird is quite willing to compromise.

Trade offs and exchanges are utilized by the Hummingbird to reach a middle ground. In other words, the Hummingbird will look for ways to give the other party part of what they want while still getting part of what the Hummingbird wants. Hummingbirds know that if they offer to give in on a certain point they are likely to get a reciprocal concession from the other party.

Amy used this tactic when she approached her employer about a salary increase. She felt that her productivity in the past year had earned her a significant salary increase and she was not hesitant in letting her employer know this. Amy told her employer exactly what she thought her salary should be. Amy's employer was noncommittal. He told her he would take her suggestion under advisement and get back to her. Amy was concerned about taking a great deal of time to work through the salary issue. She believed that her employer's hesitation was just another way of saying no. As a Hummingbird, she was more concerned that she should negotiate some kind of deal with her employer even if she didn't get the salary increase she thought she deserved. Rather than backing off and allowing her employer too much time to consider the issue, Amy came back with several options to the salary increase she originally requested. These options included a lower percentage increase, a small increase with increased vacation time, or a small increase and a title promotion. Amy thought by offering possible options to her employer, he would be more willing to meet her halfway and they could work out some sort of an agreement. To Amy, an agreement, even if it wasn't exactly what she wanted, was better than no agreement.

Compensation

For Hummingbirds, compensation is also seen as a means to an end. To get a quick solution to a problem where a compromise is not possible or feasible, finding an alternative facilitates a resolution that partially satisfies both parties. For Hummingbirds, this is not seen as giving in. Rather, Hummingbirds compensate the other party to gain an advantage. By compensating the other party, Hummingbirds look as if they have given in to the other party but in reality they are keeping the option of later exchange open. To the Hummingbird, compensation maintains negotiability and keeps communication open for the next conflict.

In union-management negotiations this tactic is frequently used. Consider what might happen when the union demands a wage increase but management refuses. Using this tactic, management might offer an alternative compensation such as a reduced work week or other benefits rather than a wage increase. This may prove satisfactory to the union because they receive some benefit from this confrontation. It also is acceptable to management because they have not given in to the demand for a wage increase. Both parties may leave this conflict somewhat satisfied. However, there is the recognition by both parties that the issue of a wage increase will have to be dealt with again at a later date.

Parents also use this tactic with their children. The household rule is no treats before dinner so when Tommy asks his mother for candy shortly before dinnertime she says no. However, Tommy's mother is aware that her son did not have his usual afternoon snack and he is probably very hungry. But she doesn't want to give in to Tommy's request for candy because of her rule regarding snacks before dinner. So she offers him carrot sticks instead. Tommy doesn't get exactly what he wants but he gets something, and his mother maintains the no treats before dinner policy.

Rationalization

Hummingbirds rely on wit to resolve conflict. They have to come up with fast and accurate rationalizations to justify their position as well as the constant shift in position. They feel that as long as they can rationalize their actions, positions, and views that the other side will concede.

Take for example, a couple going out for dinner. One person suggests that they go to an Indian restaurant for dinner. But the other person, a Hummingbird, doesn't want Indian food. Rather than saying he doesn't want that type of dinner, a Hummingbird using the rationalization tactic would start giving reasons for going to another restaurant that he would prefer. "The Indian restaurant is too far, there's another restaurant right here," or "This restaurant is much more reasonably priced than the Indian restaurant." Hummingbirds using this tactic don't say that they don't want what the other person wants nor do they firmly state what they would prefer. They give rationalizations that encourage the other party to consider other options.

Consolidation

Hummingbirds are often difficult to figure out. They may seem willing to engage and work through a conflict and then suddenly switch positions. To the other party it may seem as if the Hummingbird has decided to walk away from the conflict. But for the Hummingbird there is a sense of constant movement. If the situation does not seem to be resolved quickly, the Hummingbird will try a different angle. And if the options presented are unsatisfactory either to the Hummingbird or the other party, the Hummingbird will take some time to try to integrate the best of the different options into another option. Hummingbirds are rarely willing to disengage and walk away from a conflict. They are more likely to look for a solution to the situation that brings together at least some of the needs of all parties.

Tracy and Fatima decided they wanted to go on a winter holiday together to the Caribbean. As they were planning their vacation, Tracy commented on the numerous choices they had for their holiday. "How will we decide where we want to go?" she wondered.

Fatima announced to Tracy that she wanted to go to Jamaica and stay at a specific resort. Fatima had heard about this resort from another friend who had been there several years ago. "Let's go to a place that someone has recommended to us," she said, "because then there won't be any surprises."

Tracy was willing to consider Jamaica but she still wanted to look into other locations in the Caribbean. There seemed to be a lot of options. Fatima became more adamant. The only place she wanted to go was the resort in Jamaica.

At this point Tracy thought that Fatima was being unreasonable. Tracy had said she was willing to consider Jamaica. It wasn't that she did not want to go to Jamaica, but she wanted them to discuss the possibilities of various locations. Fatima did not budge on her position. Tracy said, "I don't think we should talk about this any more," and left.

Fatima knew that she had upset Tracy and believed that Tracy had decided she no longer wanted to go on a vacation together. However, several days later, when the two women met, Tracy brought a brochure with her. "I've found this great cruise of the Caribbean. We could spend a few days in Jamaica and then visit several other locations as well. I think this is the answer for both of us." As a Hummingbird, Tracy kept looking for options. Even when Fatima was adamant about what she wanted to do and it did not coincide with what Tracy wanted to do, Tracy kept generating options. When she found an option that she believed addressed both of their needs to some extent, Tracy was sure that she had found the perfect solution.

Brainstorming

Hummingbirds are known to put out *trial balloons* when it comes to conflict. The Hummingbird will present a hypothetical situation. "If I do this, would you agree to that?" or "If you say yes, I would probably be able to agree to that." Usually the Hummingbird will put out multiple scenarios. These brainstorming ideas are not commitments on the Hummingbird's part. They are simply options to be considered, depending on the other party's response.

Derrick and Fred were colleagues who frequently worked together on projects. Derrick realized that Fred was swamped with a variety of deadlines but he needed Fred's expertise to finish a report that was due in two days. When Derrick approached Fred to ask for his help, Fred just laughed. "You must be joking," he said. "I don't have time for any more than I've already got. I'm working on six different deadlines here. Your emergency is not my problem."

Derrick, a Hummingbird, responded by suggesting several possible solutions. "If I helped you finish some of your other projects, could you help me with this report? Or if I talk to the supervisor and negotiate an extension on your deadlines for the other projects, can you help me with this report now? Maybe I could see if Sally and Molly could take over those other projects you've got and then you could help me finish this report."

Hummingbirds like options and so will frequently provide several scenarios that will meet some of their needs and also some of the needs of the other party. This allows for room to choose and room to negotiate.

The Hummingbird's Motivation

What Hummingbirds want most of all is to work through the conflict and find a solution as quickly as possible. While to others it might appear that Hummingbirds will do almost anything in order to reach agreement, there are some basic needs motivating Hummingbirds to behave as they do.

Reciprocity

One of the Hummingbird's fundamental motivations is reciprocity. Hummingbirds want to be treated with the same respect that they have for the other party. For Hummingbirds this means negotiating with the other party. Hummingbirds believe that, by the very fact that they are willing to engage in negotiation with another, Hummingbirds are showing respect and value for the other person. Hummingbirds want to be valued and respected in return. In other words, Hummingbirds want the other party to be equally negotiable.

To a Hummingbird, being reasonable is paramount. It supersedes being right. The Hummingbird will compromise with the other party because it is reasonable. For the Hummingbird, part of being reasonable is making sure that both parties are involved in the resolution of conflict. The Hummingbird wants an exchange of opinions, ideas, options, and solutions. Throughout this exchange, the Hummingbird is always looking for some middle ground that both parties can agree on.

Hummingbirds are perfectly willing to adjust their position and demands in order to reach an agreement so long as the other party does the same. This reciprocity is not a sense of *tit for tat* for the Hummingbird. It is about being reasonable. The Hummingbird is always willing to give in to some of the other party's demands or expectations but the Hummingbird expects to receive something in return.

Choices

The Hummingbird needs choices. The Hummingbird feels hemmed in when the other party makes demands that are non-negotiable. For the Hummingbird this means that the other party is unwilling to find a middle ground. And when there is no compromise, the Hummingbird can see no positive outcome to the conflict.

For the Hummingbird there is never only one way to resolve a conflict. For this reason, the Hummingbird will constantly provide the other party with options for resolution. The Hummingbird will also respond favorably if the other party offers choices and options. When Hummingbirds do not receive such courtesies they become agitated and frustrated.

What To Expect
When You're A Hummingbird

Sidetracking

For the Hummingbird, being perceived as fair and reasonable is of great importance. The Hummingbird is always open to negotiation on issues and willing to meet the other party halfway. Hummingbirds enjoy the quick give and take of conflict and take pleasure in the process of finding a solution to the problem.

When the other party is not as negotiable as the Hummingbird, the Hummingbird experiences extreme frustration. Hummingbirds do not understand the other party's lack of reasonableness when they have so clearly demonstrated their own willingness to compromise. And, by being so unfair, the other party slows down the whole process of working through the conflict. For this reason, Hummingbirds will likely try to generate even more options for the other party in an attempt to find something that the other party might agree to. Sometimes these options or trade offs have very little to do with the conflict itself and actually sidetrack the conflict.

Maureen told us about an argument she had with her husband about their bathroom renovations. They could not agree on which tile and flooring to install. Maureen wanted a very classic look. Her husband preferred contemporary. Maureen, a Hummingbird, wanted to prove how reasonable she could be and she found some tile that she believed was somewhere between classic and contemporary. Her husband was adamant about the tile he preferred. Maureen and her husband went back and forth several times with Maureen suggesting numerous different tiles and her husband insisting on his initial choice. "Finally the only way to resolve it" said Maureen "was to agree to his tile choice in exchange for a weekend away in the fall."

Faced with her husband's unwillingness to compromise on his tile choice, Maureen had continued to provide options for resolution. She couldn't find one that her husband would agree to until she suggested the weekend away in exchange for his tile preference. Their weekend away had nothing to do with the issue of the tiles but this way Maureen could feel like they had negotiated a mutually satisfactory resolution.

Lack of Sincerity

When Hummingbirds are so quick to negotiate in a conflict situation, those who deal with Hummingbirds often question their sincerity. Many who have experienced conflict with Hummingbirds report that they find it difficult to understand what is really important to the Hummingbird.

When Hummingbirds continuously offer more options and new ideas in an attempt to come to quick resolution, they can come across as being calculating and manipulative. Their actions can be interpreted as lacking sincerity because the Hummingbird seems so willing to adapt and adjust to meet the needs of the other party. The other person is left thinking "If this was really important to him, he wouldn't be willing to compromise so quickly."

Those who are Hummingbirds may find that the other party does not see the fairness in the way they approach conflict. Rather, the other party sees the Hummingbird's behavior as taking shortcuts and bending the rules in order to reach a quick settlement. The other party can become overwhelmed by the Hummingbird and feel railroaded into agreement, not because it's right but because it's easy.

Recurrence

When a compromise is reached, it means that the issue is settled for the moment. If the conflict is complex or long-standing, however, a quick compromise rarely survives in the long term. Most conflicts settled in the Hummingbird style will show up to be dealt with again at a later date.

This can be extremely annoying to the party in conflict with the Hummingbird. But to the Hummingbird, recurrence is expected and anticipated. In fact, many of the Hummingbird's tactics are used in anticipation of the opportunity to renegotiate the issue. So the Hummingbird may be willing to go along with her spouse's plans to go fishing even when she doesn't particularly want to go fishing; with the expectation that the next time they disagree on how to spend the weekend, her spouse will allow her to chose the activity.

Two Partial Winners

The Hummingbird style is all about reaching a middle ground or compromise. With a compromise, the parties involved in the conflict end up with something that satisfies them, at least in part. The response to a compromise is usually "I can live with that." Neither party is left empty-handed. So each party wins, at least partially.

But if the parties are only partial winners it means they are also partial losers. For this reason, the two parties will likely have to deal with the same or similar issues in the future.

When To Be A Hummingbird

When The Conflict Has Turned Angry And Hostile

Conflicts can be emotional. Both parties can become angry and say things that they regret. When conflicts escalate to this extent it can be very difficult for either party to coherently talk through their differences or completely understand the other person's point of view.

In such conflict situations, utilizing a Hummingbird approach can be very useful. Conceding on a particular point or showing willingness to compromise can allow both parties to calm down. It is an opportunity to show the other party that there is room for negotiation. If the other party sees the potential for resolution, their anxiety can be alleviated and they may be more willing to engage in dialogue.

When You Need To Establish Goodwill

Most of our conflicts occur with people that we will have to deal with again in the future. In this type of situation it is not wise to burn any bridges – especially if a compromise can be reached.

If you find yourself in conflict with someone and you know that you will have other issues to work through in the future, using some Hummingbird tactics can build rapport and a sense of goodwill. The other party sees that you are willing to work together towards a solution. This puts you in a good position to work through future issues in a more positive way.

When Several Parties Are Involved

Conflicts become more complex when several parties are involved. It becomes increasingly difficult to find a solution to the problem that completely addresses the concerns of all involved. The Hummingbird approach can be useful here because it seeks to find middle ground. When there are a number of different perspectives, it may be possible to find a solution that allows everyone to come away feeling that they can live with the solution even if it is not entirely what they wanted in the beginning.

You Don't Have To Be A Hummingbird All The Time

It may be difficult to understand that the Hummingbird style is not effective in all conflict situations. But if you tend to use the Hummingbird approach in all conflict situations you have likely found that you are dealing with conflict on a fairly regular basis – with the same people and about the same issues. And it may surprise you to realize that not everyone that you have conflicts with enjoys your exchanges as much as you do.

As a Hummingbird, there are a few points that you should be aware of. It may mean that you will need to curtail your Hummingbird tendencies on occasion in order to resolve conflict more effectively.

Some Things Are Not Negotiable

Even if you believe that almost everything in life is negotiable, there are some absolutes. Everyone has values and interests that they are unwilling to compromise. As a Hummingbird, you too have some lines that you will not cross. Recognize that the other party has some absolutes as well.

We are often surprised when conflicts touch the core values of the other party. Be aware that sometimes when the other party seems to be non-negotiable it is because you are too close to something that is extremely important to them. Respect those things that are too important to compromise on and take the time to find a better solution.

Don't Assume Everyone Enjoys Negotiating

Hummingbirds enjoy the back and forth of trying to negotiate a resolution to a conflict. But negotiating is not energizing for everyone. Many individuals find the process to be draining and even nerve-racking. Recognize that it takes a great deal of effort on the part of some people to engage in the process of resolving conflict. They may not wish to explore and develop options at the same pace or with the same enthusiasm as you do. This does not mean that they are unwilling to resolve the conflict. You may need to be patient as the other party tries to communicate their interests and as they try to understand yours. It may not move as swiftly as you would like.

Don't Lose Sight Of The Real Issues

Hummingbirds are notorious for focusing on solutions quickly. Even before the issues are really clear in everyone's mind, the Hummingbird is articulating possible options for resolution. By focusing on solutions too soon, you may lose sight of the magnitude and complexity of the problem. When this happens, the options provided by the Hummingbird won't be acceptable because they won't address the underlying issues. Keep the real conflict in focus – make sure you understand what the problem is and why it is important to the other party before you start solving the problem.

Charlene often used a Hummingbird approach with her children. Both of Charlene's children loved Oreo cookies. When they were down to the last cookie in the house, Charlene heard the children arguing about who should get it. Charlene, determined to quickly break up the fight, walked into the room, took the cookie, broke it in half and gave each child half of the cookie. The children were still upset. "What's wrong now?" Charlene asked. "At least you've each got half a cookie. That's better than none at all."

"But I wanted the black part on the outside!" one child said.

"And I wanted the white stuff in the middle!" said the other.

Hummingbirds are so quick to find a compromise solution to a conflict that they may not take the time to find out exactly what the other party wants. Sometimes, with a little more discussion, they would find out that all the interests of both parties could be addressed. Make sure you know what it is that the other party wants or needs.

Limit Your Options

Using the Hummingbird conflict management style can have the opposite effect from what you want. If you seem to be negotiable about everything, the other party may perceive you as unable to take a clear stand or position. Rather than making you look more reasonable, this may damage your credibility. And if the other party doesn't respect you, they won't want to negotiate with you. Ultimately, by trying to keep all of your options open, you've limited them.

Take Your Time

Hummingbirds sometimes work through conflict situations as if there's a time pressure driving them. But taking a little more time to work through all aspects of the issue will not jeopardize the process. In fact, with a little more time and a more in-depth understanding of the issues, you are more likely to find a long-term solution to the problem rather than just a short-term settlement.

Tips For Dealing With Hummingbirds

Communicate

You need to keep the lines of communication open at all times when dealing with Hummingbirds. Because Hummingbirds move so quickly in trying to find a mutually satisfactory compromise to any conflict, it is easy to feel forced into an agreement before you are ready. Be aware of this so that you are more prepared to concentrate on the problem at hand and deal with it in its entirety. It may be up to you to bring out the larger issues or the broader implications of the current situation.

Hummingbirds do not spend a great deal of time analyzing why the conflict has occurred. You may need to help the Hummingbird understand what has happened to bring you to this point of disagreement. As the Hummingbird considers options for resolving the situation, make sure that you are considering the long-term implications of your agreement. Talk to Hummingbirds. Tell them your concerns. Hummingbirds will want to address them.

Be quick

Hummingbirds are always ready to deal with conflict. They are not intimidated by it. However, if you want to make sure the Hummingbird hears what you have to say, you will have to be quick. The Hummingbird will want to talk about how to resolve the conflict rather than the issues themselves. If you need to confront a Hummingbird, make sure you are prepared with your issues and concerns firmly and clearly in mind.

Give Options

The Hummingbird style is all about options. When you are dealing with a Hummingbird it is important that you give some consideration to the options that the Hummingbird presents to you. In the Hummingbird's mind, this means that you are interested in resolving the conflict.

Just because the Hummingbird presents you with a number of options doesn't mean you must agree to any one of them. You can present options of your own. The Hummingbird will appreciate your effort. But remember, stating one alternate solution is not giving the Hummingbird options. If you only offer one solution the Hummingbird will have the impression that you are non-negotiable and will become frustrated.

Do Not Assume The Hummingbird's Interests

When in conflict with Hummingbirds you may find their constant shifting of position confusing. Remember that when the Hummingbird gives options or presents ideas, this does not necessarily represent the interests of the Hummingbird. The Hummingbird is simply trying to find out what it is important to you so that you can begin to negotiate. In order to find out what the Hummingbird's interests are you will have to ask in a very clear and direct way.

State Your Desire For Fairness

The Hummingbird wants to know that you are in this together and that you too are attempting to resolve the conflict. If you find negotiating with a Hummingbird difficult it may be important to tell the Hummingbird that you do indeed want to find a solution to your problem. Remind the Hummingbird that you are trying to be reasonable and fair and ask the Hummingbird for the time you need. Hummingbirds will be more patient if they know that your goal is to come to a mutually satisfactory solution.

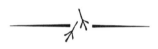

8

FLIGHT PATTERNS

The Interaction of Conflict Management Styles

What Are Flight Patterns?

As you explore your conflict management style you may find what appear to be inconsistencies in your behavior. Perhaps you find yourself behaving as a Hummingbird at work but at home you're more frequently a Woodpecker. Or you find that your Parakeet tendencies come out when you are in conflict with your mother but with your spouse you are an Owl. You may even find that when you are in conflict with someone you don't maintain the same conflict management style throughout the entire conflict. Perhaps you start out as an Ostrich but your avoidance of the issue doesn't last long and you shift to one of the other conflict management styles.

This is not unusual. Most of us don't use only one conflict management style. Your scores to the questionnaire in chapter three reflect your experience, comfort or utilization of the different conflict management styles. Any scores that are relatively close (within ten points) to your highest score indicate that you are comfortable with or have experience with these conflict management styles.

Look at the following examples. Person A is a Hummingbird. But his Owl, Woodpecker and Ostrich scores are quite close to his highest score. This person tends to approach conflict as a Hummingbird but he also will behave as an Owl, Woodpecker, or Ostrich on occasion. Person B is a Parakeet. Her next highest score, the Ostrich, is fifteen points away. All of her other scores are significantly lower. Person B approaches conflict as a Parakeet. Likely this person rarely approaches conflict in any other way. On occasion she may find herself behaving like an Ostrich but probably she rarely utilizes the other conflict management styles.

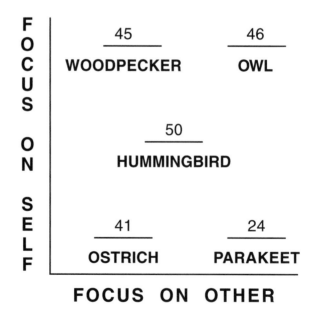

Person A

F O C U S	45 — **WOODPECKER**	46 — **OWL**
O N	50 — **HUMMINGBIRD**	
S E L F	41 — **OSTRICH**	24 — **PARAKEET**

FOCUS ON OTHER

Person B

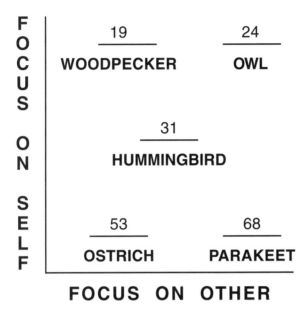

Most of us have more than one conflict management style that we utilize frequently. We move from one conflict management style to another. The way we move from one style to another takes on a certain pattern. It's called our *flight pattern*. When we find ourselves adopting different conflict management styles in different situations or with different people we are actually moving through our flight patterns.

Your flight pattern is revealed in your questionnaire scores. Your highest score indicates your preferred conflict management style. Your second highest score is the conflict management style you are likely to *fly* to next. This pattern continues from your highest score to your lowest score.

Consider Persons A and B and the questionnaire results shown earlier. Person A's flight pattern would look like this:

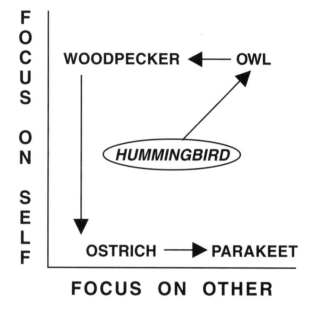

Person B's flight pattern would look like this:

Everyone has his or her own flight patterns. To determine your flight pattern, simply enter your questionnaire scores in the appropriate spots on the following grid. Circle your highest score and draw an arrow from your highest score to your second highest, then your third and so on. This is your flight pattern.

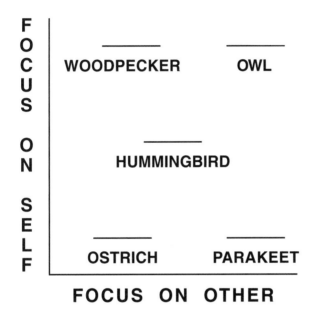

Why We Fly

Now that you've determined the direction that your flight tends to take, it is important to understand why the move from one conflict management style to another happens. We fly from one conflict management style to another for a fairly simple reason – the conflict management style we are utilizing simply isn't working for us.

Your conflict management style may be that of an Ostrich. Your preference is to avoid and ignore conflict as much as possible. If you become involved in a conflict that you can no longer avoid, you will move to another conflict management style. Which conflict management style you adopt next will, of course, depend on your flight pattern.

The same can be said of any of the other conflict management styles. You have a preferred or dominant conflict management style. This is the way you will initially respond to conflict. There will be occasions, however, when the party you are in conflict with will respond in such a way that you simply cannot maintain your preferred conflict management style.

The incentive for movement comes from the reaction of the party you are in conflict with. If you are a Woodpecker and the other party responds to you in such a way that you find you cannot possibly win the argument, you will fly to another conflict management style. This is because the Woodpecker's purpose or goal is to be the victor. The Parakeet's goal, however, is to allow the other person to win in order to maintain a harmonious relationship. So if the Parakeet is involved in a conflict where the other party responds in such a way that the Parakeet's style cannot achieve this goal, the Parakeet will fly to another style. For the Owl, flight occurs when the other party is unwilling to engage in the process of slowly working through all issues and collaborating on a solution. The Ostrich, as we said earlier, will fly to another conflict management style when the conflict can no longer be avoided. The Hummingbird will fly to another style when the offer to negotiate and compromise on a solution has been consistently rebuffed.

Movement from one conflict management style to another does not guarantee success in dealing with the conflict. If you move to another conflict management style and find that style isn't getting the desired results you will continue to move through your flight pattern.

It should be noted that for most of the conflict management styles, an initial lack of response from the other party does not mean that you will immediately move on to the next style in your flight pattern. There are certainly occasions when, if the other party seems uncooperative with our conflict management style, we actually become more firmly entrenched in our behavior. Woodpeckers who do not get quick agreement from the other party will not immediately fly to another conflict management style. Rather they will become more determined to make their point. Flight to another style only comes after the Woodpecker has become extremely disturbed by the other party's unwillingness to see things from the Woodpecker's point of view. The same can be said of all of the conflict management styles. Flight to another style is not necessarily quick and usually only happens after a great deal of energy has been invested and extreme frustration has been experienced because of the other party's behavior.

Intersections

Because of our flight patterns, our interactions with other people take on certain patterns. Have you noticed that the conflicts you experience with one person don't necessarily follow the same pattern as the conflicts you experience with someone else? Your flight pattern intersects the flight pattern of whomever you are in conflict with. With some people you will find yourself flying swiftly from one conflict management style to another. Not just because of your flight pattern but because of their flight pattern as well. With other people you may find that you use only your preferred style and rarely have a need to fly to another mode of behavior.

Let's look at an example. Nathan is married to Samantha. This is Nathan's flight pattern:

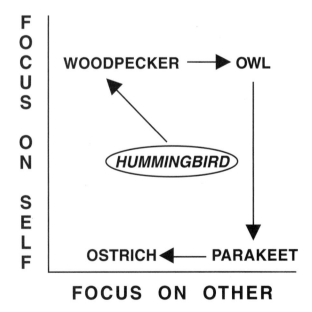

This is Samantha's flight pattern:

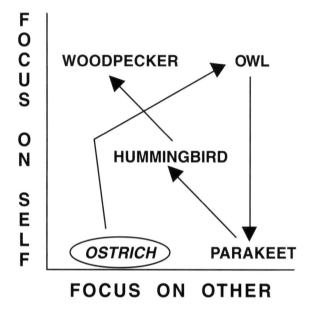

When Nathan and Samantha experience conflict, the pattern goes something like this: Nathan will notice that something seems to be upsetting Samantha and starts asking questions. Samantha insists that nothing is wrong and that she doesn't want to talk about it (Ostrich). Nathan will continue to ask questions because he knows that something is going on. He will provide options as if it is a multiple-choice question (Hummingbird), "Is this what's bothering you? Are you upset about that? Is it something I did? Did you want someone to do that?" Samantha will continue in her Ostrich behavior and insist that she just wants to be left alone.

In frustration, because Samantha has not responded to any of his options, Nathan's behavior changes. "Okay," he says, "I'm doing this my way." (Woodpecker). Now Samantha's frustration mounts. She didn't want to talk about it but now that Nathan is insisting on doing things his way, she knows she cannot avoid the issue any longer. "We need to talk about this," she says to Nathan. "Why do you want to do it that way? What are you hoping to accomplish? Why haven't you asked me what I want?" (Owl).

Here is where the conflict may move in two different directions. Samantha's Owl tactics and insistence on talking about the situation may annoy Nathan to the point where he stubbornly remains in Woodpecker mode. "I did ask you, over and over again and you insisted that you had no opinion!"

Or, Samantha's Owl behavior may mean that Nathan will never get Samantha's agreement until they discuss things. If this is the case, Nathan will fly to the Owl style. When both Samantha and Nathan are Owls, the situation gets thoroughly discussed. They stay up all night or spend several days talking and analyzing what happened and why they responded as they did. Eventually they will find a mutually satisfying resolution.

If Nathan maintains his Woodpecker position however, Samantha will not remain an Owl. She becomes frustrated because Nathan is unwilling to consider her perspective or look at another way of resolving the situation. Annoyed, Samantha moves in her flight pattern to the Parakeet style. Here she gives in to Nathan and says, "Okay, okay. Do it your way."

Samantha and Nathan admit that they can map out almost every conflict they have ever experienced as moving through one of these two patterns. "I don't ever recall," says Samantha, "a time when we made a quick compromise, and resolved a conflict between us with a little give and take." They have never both used the Hummingbird conflict management style to resolve issues together. This is because Nathan will start in this mode while it is one of Samantha's least used conflict management styles. Nathan would simply not remain in Hummingbird mode long enough for Samantha to move through her flight pattern to the Hummingbird style.

Nathan will also point out that conflicts don't get avoided in their relationship either. Although this is Samantha's preferred way of dealing with conflict, it is Nathan's least preferred conflict management style. There are many other tactics Nathan will try in a variety of different conflict management styles before Nathan would be willing to ignore the conflict. Because he won't avoid it, Samantha usually can't either.

Samantha reports that her conflicts with her sister take on a very different pattern. Her sister is an Ostrich just like Samantha. "I would have initially said that my sister and I never have conflict," said Samantha "but that's not entirely true. I do remember some occasions when I was really upset by something she said or did. But I would never confront her with it. And she would never challenge me. We just carry on and pretend it never happened. We've never talked about our differences."

For Samantha and her sister there is no need to fly to another conflict management style. By utilizing their preferred style, the Ostrich, each is able to avoid the conflict. Since this seems to meet both of their needs, neither will move to another conflict management style. It is possible, of course, that avoiding conflicts will not work all the time for Samantha and her sister. They may experience serious differences at some point that require them to acknowledge the situation and discuss it. At this point, their flight patterns will come into play.

Nathan also sees a marked difference between how he works through conflict with Samantha and how he works through conflict with his colleague, Jeff. Jeff's flight pattern looks like this:

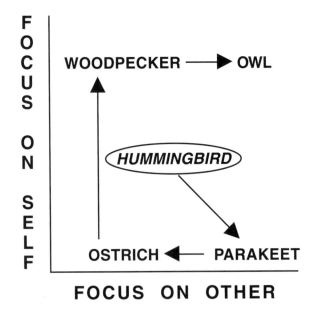

When Nathan and Jeff have a difference of opinion, it is usually very short-lived. Because they both prefer the Hummingbird style, a quick compromise is usually their immediate response to conflict. They negotiate a bit, meet each other half way and move on. There is no need to utilize any other conflict management style in this scenario.

On occasion, however, the issue causing the conflict is one in which a quick compromise cannot be reached. They may try to find a middle ground but they are unable to find a quick solution. In this case, Nathan will move to the Woodpecker style. He becomes insistent on making his point of view clear and wants Jeff to agree with him. Jeff flies to the Parakeet style. At this point he usually gives in and lets Nathan do things his way.

It is important to remember that our flight patterns are not something we consciously choose. Just like our dominant conflict management style, our flight pattern happens when we are more or less on automatic pilot. Flight patterns can also be influenced by our experiences, the way we've learned to deal with conflict, or the conflict management styles that have been modeled for us. But our flight pattern is all a part of the knee jerk reaction that is our response to conflict.

We also need to recognize that as our flight patterns intersect, certain conflict management styles will meet and others will collide. There are five conflict management styles. This means that there are fifteen possible combinations of conflict management styles when two individuals are in conflict. In some cases, the pairing of conflict management styles allows for the possibility of an end to the conflict or at least an end to the current confrontation. In other cases, the pairing is so volatile that nothing can be resolved unless one or both parties moves on to the next conflict management style.

Let's take a look at what to expect in each possible combination of conflict management styles.

Woodpecker – Owl

Woodpeckers focus on decisive action. Owls focus on process. When these two conflict management styles meet Woodpeckers will dig in their heels and obstinately stick to their position. They see Owls as postponing the inevitable or, at worst, as obstructionists who don't want resolution because they continue to want to explore issues and talk things through.

Owls, on the other hand, look at Woodpeckers as one-sided and non-cooperative. Owls see themselves as reasonable and fair and see the Woodpecker as the opposite – unreasonable and unfair.

As these two interact, Woodpeckers will stick stubbornly to their position and Owls will keep asking why. "Why is this your position?" "Why won't you move?" "Why won't you consider something else?" "Why won't you listen to reason?"

Woodpeckers will often interpret such questions as an attempt to find fault with the Woodpecker's reasoning. If this happens, Woodpeckers will actually become less communicative and less willing to explain their position. Their responses become "Because." "Because this is what I think." "Because this is what I want to do." "Because it is."

As you can see, no resolution will be found if this continues. Therefore either one or both will need to move to another conflict management style before there is a sense of resolution.

Woodpecker – Hummingbird

Woodpeckers usually don't trust Hummingbirds. Hummingbirds can look manipulative and calculating because they can't be pinned down to a specific, concrete position. As long as the Hummingbird does not take a firm stand on the issue, the Woodpecker will be suspicious of the Hummingbird's motives.

The Hummingbird sees the Woodpecker's firm position as a challenge. Hummingbirds will attempt to manipulate Woodpeckers and lead them to a specific resolution. The Hummingbird will allow the Woodpecker to believe that the Woodpecker has won the conflict but will get the Woodpecker to a position that is acceptable to the Hummingbird as well.

When a Woodpecker and Hummingbird are in conflict, the conflict can be resolved without movement to other conflict management styles. The result will be, however, a winner and a loser.

Who the winner is and who the loser is will not always be clear. This will depend on the Hummingbird's negotiating strength. When Hummingbirds are strong negotiators they can use their skills to steer Woodpeckers into a position that is a compromise without the Woodpecker even realizing it. In other words, Hummingbirds may suggest options for resolution but do so in such a way that Woodpeckers think it is their idea. Hummingbirds may even act as if they don't want this resolution so that the Woodpecker adheres more firmly to the idea. In such a situation both the Hummingbird and the Woodpecker believe that they have won.

If the Hummingbird is not a skilled negotiator or the Woodpecker wields more power than the Hummingbird, Woodpeckers may simply squash the Hummingbird's ideas to get their way. Once again there is a winner and a loser. In this situation, however, it is very clear who has won and who has lost.

Woodpecker – Parakeet

With this combination, there is an end to the conflict, at least on the surface. Woodpeckers will get their way and Parakeets will agree with the Woodpeckers. The Parakeet will usually feel resentful or taken for granted but will continue to appease the Woodpecker in any way possible.

In this type of scenario, Woodpeckers rarely realize that their behavior has caused pain or frustration to the Parakeets because the Parakeets will not clearly say so. As long as Parakeets maintain this conflict management style and give in to Woodpeckers, there is no incentive for the Woodpeckers to move to another conflict management style because they are getting their way.

The danger with this combination occurs when *all* conflicts between two individuals are resolved in this way. If this pattern is sustained over a long period of time it can result in dysfunction. If one party gives in to the other party in every conflict they encounter, there is no reciprocity in the relationship. Then, if at some point the Parakeet becomes disillusioned and moves to another conflict management style, the relationship may not be able to sustain any other way of handling conflict. It may mean the end of the relationship.

This is not to say that this combination never works. If conflicts are occasionally resolved with one person using a Woodpecker style and the other using a Parakeet style it can actually be a sign of a healthy and dynamic relationship. Remember that the Parakeet considers the relationship with the other party to be paramount. There are occasions when the contentious issue is much more significant to the Woodpecker than the Parakeet. The Parakeet, recognizing the importance of preserving the relationship, gives in to the Woodpecker. In healthy relationships, either partner may occasionally find themselves behaving as a Parakeet while the other is behaving as a Woodpecker.

Woodpecker – Ostrich

When a Woodpecker and Ostrich have differences there is usually a delay in the actual conflict. For example, a parent tells her teenager that he must have his room clean by the time she returns from work. The Woodpecker parent is very clear with her son. "I want this room neat and tidy by the time I get back." The Ostrich teenager doesn't look his mother in the eye. Under his breath he says, "Whatever."

If you would ask that Woodpecker parent what she expects to find when she gets home she would say that she expects her son's room to be clean. The Ostrich teenager, however, would likely say that he made no commitment to his mother.

The actual confrontation occurs when the parent returns home and the teenager's room is not cleaned. The Woodpecker parent will loudly demand answers as to why the room is not clean. The Ostrich teenager will not engage. If possible, he will physically remove himself from the situation.

The more the Woodpecker insists on a specific outcome the more reticent the Ostrich will become. With this combination, there will be no resolution until one or both parties move to another conflict management style.

Woodpecker – Woodpecker

This combination is a nonstarter in a sense. For both Woodpeckers, power is the vehicle to achieve their goals. If the Woodpeckers are the quiet type, there will be a battle of one-upmanship. Each will try to weaken the other's argument and gain the advantage. If the Woodpeckers are the loud type, this conflict may get *very* loud.

Unlike the back and forth of a tennis match, this confrontation is more likely to look like a constant barrage from both sides. There will be no give and take. Each Woodpecker will be more interested in the virtues of his own argument. Both will be tearing down the other's position and pointing out the virtues of their own position. There is no attempt to understand each other or to offer any openings for negotiation.

Occasionally this type of battle will end with a clear winner and loser. But if one Woodpecker wins, the victory is short lived. The loser will immediately be thinking about what he needs to do to win the next battle. The mentality is one of an ongoing war.

More likely, this combination won't end the conflict and there will only be a sense of resolution if there is movement by one or both parties.

Owl – Hummingbird

When an Owl and Hummingbird experience conflict there is a possibility for resolution, but it doesn't always happen. The challenge with this combination is that the Hummingbird would like to expedite things and move quickly towards resolution. The Owl is concerned with the process and making sure all aspects of the situation have been adequately explored. The Hummingbird will likely get frustrated with the time the Owl wants to take to resolve the situation.

Where Hummingbirds want to be reasonable, Owls want to be fair. Hummingbirds are likely to provide a number of possible solutions to the conflict that they perceive as reasonable. Owls, however, will need time to evaluate these options to determine if they are really fair. Resolution of the conflict is possible if the Owl considers one of the *reasonable* options presented by the Hummingbird as *fair*. If the Owl finds a suggestion for resolution made by the Hummingbird addresses both of their concerns entirely then the Owl will accept this resolution. It rarely happens the other way around, however. The Owl is not likely to make a suggestion that is agreeable to the Hummingbird. Owls will simply not move to a discussion of solutions as quickly as Hummingbirds.

When a conflict is ongoing between an Owl and a Hummingbird, their desire to be fair and to be reasonable will likely result in some movement toward each other's comfort zone. Owls may agree to forgo a lengthy analysis of the situation with the justification that they must do so in order to meet the needs of Hummingbirds. Owls will perceive this as a *fair* movement on their part. Hummingbirds may take a little more time to work through things with Owls, recognizing the opportunity to negotiate different aspects of the conflict. Hummingbirds will perceive this movement as *reasonable*. Neither party will see this as flying to another conflict management style but it will provide the opportunity for resolution.

Owl – Ostrich

As is so well demonstrated by the grid, these two conflict management styles are complete opposites. The Owl has a need for extensive communication, details, information and the response of the other party. The Ostrich will not respond at all. Therefore the combination of these two conflict management styles will only lead to frustration and the conflict will not be resolved at this point.

This particular combination is very challenging. The Ostrich is likely to say, "If you think we have a problem, you solve it," which doesn't work for the Owl at all. There will be no resolution without movement by one or both parties.

Owl – Parakeet

When an Owl and a Parakeet are in conflict, the process of working through the conflict will always be cordial. Noisy outbursts or stony silences are unlikely to occur.

The Owl will find the Parakeet's tactics somewhat challenging. The Owl will continually be eliciting feedback from the Parakeet. The Owl will want to understand the Parakeet's point of view and will want to know the Parakeet's needs or expectations. The Parakeet, on the other hand, will attempt to minimize the situation and emphasize the positive aspects of the relationship. While the Owl will not disagree with the Parakeet, the Owl will want to go beyond this to talk about their differences. The Parakeet will continue to focus on their similarities.

Occasionally an Owl and a Parakeet will be able to resolve their conflict at this point. If the issue is largely a relational one, the Parakeet's ability to concentrate on their points of agreement may satisfy the Owl's need to analyze the situation.

Frequently, however, the Parakeet's tactics will frustrate the Owl. The Owl wants to build a dialogue with the Parakeet and so may try to articulate both points of view in order to do so. Owls may actually build the Parakeet's argument for them. In such a situation Owls may put words in the Parakeet's mouth. If the Owl is accurate in describing the Parakeet's concerns, it may be the Parakeet who flies to another conflict management style.

Owl – Owl

When two Owls experience conflict, resolution is achievable but the process will be lengthy and time-consuming. Both Owls will want to understand the conflict in a detailed and comprehensive way. All possible solutions will be thoroughly analyzed.

It may be assumed that the best way to resolve any conflict is when both parties are utilizing the Owl conflict management style. If the issues of a conflict are significant to both parties and the relationship between the two parties is also important, this combination of styles may be able to find an appropriate resolution.

But there are challenges that come with this combination as well. When there is mutual respect between the two Owls, a dialogue will develop. If, however, one Owl has greater communication skills than the other, a sense of competition may result. If each Owl does not value the other's perspective, one may believe they have a better answer than the other does.

Two Owls will take an exceptionally long time to resolve a conflict. While both parties may be willing to invest their time, the situation may have external time constraints. In such a situation the two Owls may find that they cannot resolve the conflict if limited time is allowed.

Hummingbird – Ostrich

With this combination the Ostrich will attempt to deny that any conflict exists while the Hummingbird, who would usually focus on a quick compromise, will want the Ostrich to admit that there is a conflict. In fact, Hummingbirds may see it as their mission to get the Ostrich to acknowledge the presence of a conflict.

Hummingbirds will utilize their tactics to maneuver Ostriches into admitting that there is a problem. The Hummingbird will offer trade offs and potential solutions to a situation that the Ostrich denies exists. For the Ostrich, the Hummingbird's behavior will feel like a minefield of traps that the Ostrich needs to run away from.

The more the Hummingbird persists, the more trapped the Ostrich will feel. The longer the Ostrich evades the Hummingbird and refuses to respond or acknowledge the conflict, the more frustrated the Hummingbird will become. In order for conflict to be resolved, one or both of the parties will need to move to another conflict management style.

Hummingbird – Parakeet

When the Hummingbird and Parakeet are in conflict, neither party is likely to allow the conflict to get ugly or out of hand. Some sort of resolution is generally possible with this combination. The Hummingbird will generate options for resolution and the Parakeet will usually be amenable to any reasonable solutions offered.

The Hummingbird will derive some satisfaction from the positive response of the Parakeet but may be skeptical of the Parakeet's quick agreement. This is because Hummingbirds use a similar tactic but for a different purpose. Hummingbirds will trade off their agreement on one issue in exchange for the other party's agreement on another issue. When Parakeets give in quickly Hummingbirds expect the Parakeet to have similar motives. Hummingbirds look for what they assume to be the Parakeet's hidden agenda.

If this carries on for too long either or both parties may move to another conflict management style.

Hummingbird – Hummingbird

Conflict between two Hummingbirds is generally quick and relatively painless. In fact, two Hummingbirds usually enjoy the lively give and take of their interactions.

When two Hummingbirds are involved in a conflict they may try to outdo each other to see who can come up with the best solution or who can come up with the most options for resolving the situation. This may prolong the conflict somewhat, but because they are enjoying the negotiations, the Hummingbirds don't mind.

Two Hummingbirds will find a compromise that they both can accept. Depending on the issues, this can be a long-lasting resolution or an interim settlement. In either case the two Hummingbirds will be satisfied and are not likely to feel the need to fly to another conflict management style.

Ostrich – Parakeet

Conflicts between an Ostrich and a Parakeet are frequently painful and messy. Parakeets will go out of their way to be helpful. They may even take full responsibility for the conflict, insisting that it is their fault. But the Ostrich will counter this with rejection, insisting instead that there is no conflict and that it's all in the Parakeet's imagination.

This rebuff by the Ostrich can seem very spiteful to the Parakeet who wants to keep their relationship pleasant and harmonious. The Parakeet's tactics, on the other hand, are smothering to the Ostrich.

If the Parakeet persists, the Ostrich may feel so trapped that there is no choice but to use their powerful kick. The Ostrich may say something personal and extremely hurtful and then walk away.

With this combination no resolution to the conflict is possible. One or both parties will need to move to another conflict management style.

Ostrich – Ostrich

No resolution is possible if two Ostriches are in conflict. This will not be troublesome to the two parties however, as they don't want to acknowledge the conflict anyway!

Resolution is only possible if one or both parties fly to another conflict management style. But with two Ostriches there is no impetus for movement. So long as both parties are ignoring their differences neither will see a need to make any changes to their behavior.

Conflict between Ostriches can be incredibly long lasting. Only when a third party or circumstances force one or both of the Ostriches to acknowledge the conflict will there be any movement to other conflict management styles.

Parakeet – Parakeet

Two Parakeets are usually able to pacify each other and achieve at least a superficial resolution to their conflict.

When two Parakeets experience conflict they will continue to be pleasant and talk around the issues. To onlookers there may be no evidence of a conflict at all. But the Parakeets know what they're talking about.

Conflict between two Parakeets can look a little bit like a dance where no one is leading. Neither party will force their position on the other and each will be quick to acknowledge the validity of the other's position. The only real question between Parakeets is who will give in to whom.

Mapping Flight Patterns

Recognizing your flight pattern and that of others whom you have conflict with can be a valuable tool in understanding your interactions. You can begin to see why conflicts are sometimes long and drawn out, volatile at other times, and relatively quick and painless in other situations.

You may want to map out your flight pattern and how it interacts with the flight patterns of your spouse, friends, or colleagues. The following charts can be used to map out additional flight patterns. Use them to analyze and understand the conflicts you experience with others.

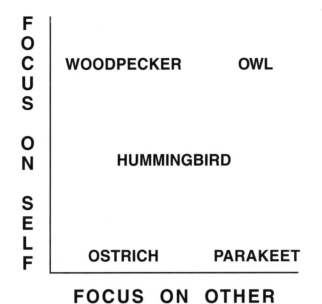

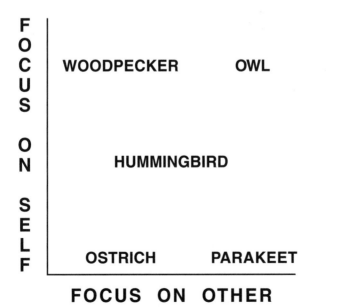

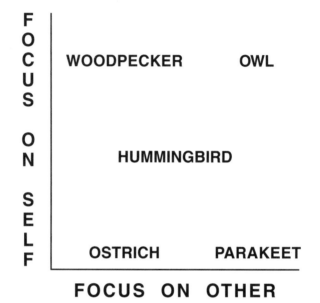

9

Managing Your Migration

Doing Conflict Differently

Barbara and Denise

Barbara and Denise were sisters. Their mother died when they were very young and their father raised the girls. They both thought the world of him. The three were a tight-knit family.

When Barbara and Denise were in their late twenties, their father passed away suddenly. Both women grieved the loss deeply.

As they began to sort through his estate, complications arose. Their father had not left a will. Barbara and Denise disagreed about what his wishes and intentions had been.

Their father had not been a wealthy man but he did have a number of antiques and some jewelry that his mother had passed down to him. His house and car were paid for and they were also a part of his estate.

Barbara and Denise agreed to meet at the house to begin sorting through their father's things. When Barbara arrived she found Denise already working.

"I've begun by putting some of these things into piles. I've made a pile of things I want to keep. All of that other stuff will go to charity unless you want some of it," said Denise.

"What do you think you're doing?" exclaimed Barbara. "You have no right to make decisions about these things all by yourself."

"Well, I know that Dad wanted me to have these. I had talked to him about it," replied Denise.

Barbara wasn't sure she believed Denise. Denise had already put most of the family jewelry and several other valuable items in *her* pile.

Barbara believed that her father would have wanted both of them to have some of the family's heirlooms.

The doorbell rang. Barbara went to greet the realtor that she had called earlier. Within minutes the "For Sale" sign was up on the front lawn and the realtor was talking about the potential buyers she had. Denise came into the room just as the realtor left, having made plans to show the house the next day.

"What is going on?" Denise asked, clearly angry.

"I've made arrangements to put the house on the market. The realtor says it will sell quickly," replied Barbara.

"But you can't sell the house. Dad wanted to keep the house in the family."

"Dad never said any such thing. Besides, neither of us is in a position to maintain a house like this. It makes more sense to sell it and split the money we get for it."

"You can't sell the house."

"It's already on the market."

"I'll call a lawyer and he'll put a stop to it. This isn't what our father wanted!"

Barbara laughed cynically. "But he wanted you to have all of Grandma's jewelry and the silver? I don't think so. I can't believe how selfish you are."

"I can't believe how unfeeling *you* are."

The two sisters, furious with each other, left the house.

Within days the realtor called Barbara. They had an offer on the house. Barbara knew she had to tell her sister about it. She phoned Denise.

"Denise, I'm selling the house. Call your lawyers if you want to but this is a great offer. We'd be fools not to take it."

"Barbara, I'm sorry I blew up the other day at the house. I guess I'm still overly emotional about all this. I don't want us to fight."

"There's nothing to fight about. I just need your signature on these papers so that we can sell the house."

Unwilling to argue any further, Denise responded, "Yes, of course."

Over the next several weeks, Barbara proceeded to sell their father's car and several of the larger antiques. Denise couldn't believe that Barbara was disposing of their father's belongings in such a heartless way without even talking to her about it.

For her part, every time she went to the house Barbara noticed things that were missing. She knew that Denise was taking these things because, as her sister said, Dad wanted her to have them. Barbara was furious with Denise. She believed that Denise was taking more than her fair share of the estate.

When Denise was couriered the final deed of sale on the house to sign, she couldn't stand it any more. She knew she needed to do something about the tension between her and her sister. Denise called Barbara.

"Barbara, we need to talk. I know you're angry with me and I'm sorry for anything I've done to upset you. But we're sisters. We're the only family each other has. We need to take care of each other – not fight."

"I don't know what you're talking about Denise. I'm not angry."

"We should have talked more about what to do with Dad's things," Denise said. "Maybe we still can. We can decide what to keep and then each take what we want. Or if there are some things you want to keep, just tell me. I know we can work things out."

"Look Denise, I've really got to go. As far as I'm concerned there's really nothing we need to talk about."

"But I just feel like I've upset you and I want to make it up to you."

"So what you're really talking about is what *you* need and how *you* feel. Typical, isn't it? Everything always seems to be about you!"

"See, Barbara, I *knew* you were upset. Can't we talk about it?"

"You know, Denise, I really have nothing else to say to you."

With that, Barbara hung up the phone.

Denise was shocked by Barbara's behavior. It was obvious that Barbara did not want to talk to her. And in a way, it just seemed easier to Denise not to talk to Barbara anymore either.

The rest of their father's estate was settled without the sisters meeting. They would send messages back and forth by courier or through mutual friends if something needed the other's signature. But they did not actually speak to each other.

The weeks of silence turned into months and then into years. In fact, Barbara and Denise did not speak to each other for over fifteen years. It was then that Denise discovered she had terminal cancer. She thought of her sister but after so many years of silence Denise didn't know how to approach Barbara. Denise passed away without seeing her sister again.

When Barbara was informed of her sister's death, she was filled with regret. Why hadn't they been able to resolve their differences?

Getting Stuck

Barbara and Denise were locked in a pattern of intersecting conflict management styles that led to frustration and ultimately, alienation. For both Barbara and Denise their flight patterns resulted in the interaction of conflict management styles that did not enable them to resolve their differences.

The two sisters both initially adopted a Woodpecker approach to the conflict. It was clear that these two styles could not come to resolution. Both women wanted the other to admit that she was wrong. And both women adamantly maintained that she had done nothing wrong.

Out of frustration Denise flew to a Parakeet style. She was not able to find an agreeable solution at this point because Barbara had adopted an Ostrich style. Further aggravated, Denise flew to a third conflict management style and she too became an Ostrich.

As Ostriches, the two women never addressed their conflict and it was never resolved. It could have been different if Barbara and Denise had chosen to deal with the conflict in a different way.

The operative word here is *chosen*. Barbara and Denise's conflict management styles were reflex reactions to a sensitive and obviously significant issue for both of them. Neither sister questioned her own behavior. Barbara and Denise reacted to the situation and to each other without considering the consequences of their responses. They didn't choose to behave differently because they didn't realize they had a choice.

When we don't make a conscious choice about our behavior we get stuck in those instinctive knee-jerk responses that we've learned and developed. We react as if we're on automatic pilot without thought for the issues of the conflict, the other party, or the results we want.

But we do have choices. When we are faced with a conflict we can choose to be a Woodpecker, Parakeet, Owl, Ostrich or Hummingbird. We don't need to be limited by our instinctive conflict management styles or our flight patterns. We can manage our migration and fly to whichever conflict management style is appropriate to the situation.

Making Choices

There are two important aspects of managing your migration. Firstly, you must be able to determine which conflict management style would be most appropriate. You do this by looking at the conflict situation. What are the issues? How important are the issues to you and the other party? How important is your relationship?

When you consider these factors you can eliminate ineffective styles and determine appropriate styles. For example, let's say you disagree with your best friend about what time you're going to meet. You suggest meeting at two because it's convenient for you but you don't have any plans that couldn't be changed to accommodate other meeting times. Your friend, however, wants to meet at four because she is under some pressure to get something done before you get together. You recognize that the issue is more important to her than to you. It really doesn't matter to you what time you meet. For her, the time is significant. For you, being a Woodpecker in this situation will not get the results you want. The issue is not important to you but it is to the other party. This is your best friend – the relationship is likely more important than meeting at a time that is most convenient to you. To insist on meeting at two in the Woodpecker style will likely result in heightened tension and further conflict. The Owl and Ostrich styles will not be the most helpful either.

This is not such a significant issue that it needs to be discussed at length like an Owl. And since you are talking about meeting your friend, to simply ignore the conflict won't work. The use of the Parakeet or Hummingbird style will likely result in a satisfactory solution and enhance a significant relationship. As a Parakeet, you can agree to meet your friend at four because you know that is the best time for her. Or, as a Hummingbird, you negotiate another option – perhaps you meet at three or suggest meeting tomorrow when both of you have a more flexible schedule.

In another example, if you disagree with your colleagues about what to do on a job that you are ultimately responsible for, a Parakeet approach may not be as useful. To simply give in to your co-workers' ideas because you don't want to have any negative feelings developing may result in a project that you cannot justify. An Ostrich approach likely wouldn't be helpful either. In the end, you are the one who is going to have to present the project to your superior and you will be asked to explain all aspects of the project. You can't claim that you knew nothing about the problems and issues that arose along the way. Depending on the actual task and the time constraints, a Woodpecker, Owl or Hummingbird approach could bring you the results you need. Perhaps the conflict between you and your co-workers could be resolved with a compromise that would satisfy everyone and allow the project to move ahead. If so, a Hummingbird approach will work. But if the issue is complex and has significant long-term ramifications, an Owl approach may allow you to find a solution that actually improves the quality of the project. And if the issue is one in which you know you are right and you have to get things done in a hurry, the Woodpecker approach may be the one to take.

When determining which conflict management style is appropriate you also need to consider the conflict management style of the other party. Your style may be an appropriate one but if it interacts negatively with the other party's conflict management style, you will not be able to resolve the issue effectively. So if you are a Parakeet when you and your best friend disagree about what time to meet but your friend is an Ostrich, your use of the Parakeet style may be appropriate to the situation but not helpful in resolving the conflict because of your friend's avoiding behavior. You may be willing to accommodate your friend's needs and change your meeting time but if your friend denies that she has any difficulty with a two o'clock meeting time, you won't be able to accommodate her. Or if you adopt the Owl style with your colleague when you disagree about how to complete a project but your colleague is a Woodpecker, although your Owl style is appropriate, the interaction with a Woodpecker may escalate the conflict rather than resolve it.

Flexibility

The other part of managing your migration is developing your ability to use all five conflict management styles. Most of us use our preferred conflict management style and maybe one or two others on a fairly frequent basis. Not many of us feel equally comfortable using all five.

Sometimes we are so stuck in our conflict management style that it seems almost impossible to consider any other behavior. In one of our workshops, participants were role-playing the five conflict management styles. One of the participants was a very strong Woodpecker and he freely admitted that he rarely used any other approach to conflict. When it was his turn to role-play another conflict management style he quickly became frustrated. The new behaviors were unnatural to him and he really didn't know how to behave or what to say as anything other than a Woodpecker.

Developing flexibility in our use of conflict management styles can take some effort. Like all important skills, it takes practice. And like all new skills, it may not be perfect the first time. If you are an Owl and you want to learn to be a Hummingbird, it may be difficult to stop asking questions and simply agree to a reasonable solution even when you know you should. But try to adjust your behavior a little at a time. Ask fewer questions and take a little less time to analyze the situation. The same goes for any of the other conflict management styles. Take a close look at your behavior in conflict situations. Recognize those tactics that you use too often. What do you need to do to eliminate or at least curb those behaviors? Then take a look at the conflict management style that you are least comfortable using. Think about the characteristics of that style. The next time you find yourself involved in a conflict where that style would be appropriate, try to use some of those tactics. Your comfort level in using all five conflict management styles will only increase by practicing and using them.

Responding Instead Of Reacting

There is a difference between reacting to conflict and responding to conflict. When we react we are acting instinctively. When we respond we are acting intentionally. Managing our migration is intentionally responding to conflict. It is recognizing that our experiences with conflict don't need to be limited by our conflict management style or our flight pattern.

Managing our migration is an opportunity for greater awareness. If we examine our conflict behaviors we will learn more about ourselves. And if we approach conflict with others in an intentional way we will discover a great deal about the other party and about our relationship with them.

Responding to conflict thoughtfully and with appropriate consideration is a key part of healthy, stable relationships. Janeen told us about her marriage to Patrick. "They say opposites attract and for us that is certainly true. It seems like we can't agree on anything – from the simplest things like who does the dishes and how to do the laundry to much more complex issues about religion, politics, and money. We experience conflict on a daily basis because we are such different people. The way he does things is just not the way I do things. And many of my priorities are meaningless to him."

Interestingly, Janeen and Patrick had been married for nearly twenty-five years when she told us this. As Janeen explained, their differences and how they chose to resolve the conflicts, those differences created were what deepened and strengthened their relationship. "We have learned that you can never make assumptions. You can't assume the other person is going to agree with you or even understand you. And you certainly can't assume that you know what is important to the other person. Every conflict is a new discovery, another opportunity to understand each other at a deeper level."

Managing our migration allows us to consider the consequences of our actions. Alfred Nobel was a Swedish inventor of various types of explosives including dynamite, blasting caps, and smokeless gunpowder. When his death was falsely reported, Alfred Nobel discovered that he would be remembered around the world as the man responsible for escalating the arms race. Alfred Nobel considered the consequences of his life's work and was unwilling to let this be his epitaph. He decided he wanted a different result and so he acted accordingly. Alfred Nobel used the wealth he had amassed from building weapons to create prizes in several areas. Today the Nobel Peace Prize is one of the most prestigious awards in the world. From weapons of war came the promotion of peace. Alfred Nobel made a choice. Rather than a legacy of destruction, he chose to leave a legacy of creativity and reconciliation.

Conflict is dynamic. It contains the potential for destruction but it also contains the potential for creation. Consider the oyster. That tiny grain of sand that finds its way into the oyster's shell is an irritant. But what does the oyster do with that irritant? It transforms that grain of sand into a pearl. The conflict we experience is an irritant. But it doesn't need to consume us, define us, or destroy us. The question is what we will do with that conflict. We can learn to transform that conflict into an experience that expands our consciousness. It can be an opportunity for growth.

The possibility of new ideas, innovative solutions and stronger relationships is there in every conflict. The key is responding to conflict appropriately and intentionally. The power to determine our own actions and work towards better solutions is ours.

Bibliography

Arnold, John D. *When the Sparks Fly: Resolving Conflict in Your Organization.* New York, NY: McGraw-Hill, Inc., 1993.

Benfari, Robert. *Changing Your Management Style.* New York, NY: Lexington Books, 1995.

Blake, Robert R. and Mouton, Jane S. *The Managerial Grid.* Houston, TX: Gul Publishing Company, 1964.

Deutsh, Morton and Coleman, Peter T., eds. *The Handbook of Conflict Resolution.* San Francisco, CA: Jossey-Bass, 2000.

Crum, Thomas F. *The Magic of Conflict.* New York, NY: Simon and Schuster, 1987.

Domenici, Kathy and Stephen W. Littlejohn. *Mediation: Empowerment in Conflict Management.* Prospect Heights, IL: Waveland Press, 1996.

Douglas, Eric F. *Straight Talk.* Palo Alto, CA: Davies-Black Publishing, 1998.

Hocker, Joyce L., and Wilmot, William W. *Interpersonal Conflict*, 4th Edition. Dubuque, IA: Brown and Benchmark Publishers, 1995.

Jandt, Fred E. *The Process of Interpersonal Communication.* San Francisco, CA: Canfield Press, 1976.

Kaufman, Gershen and Raphael, Lev. *The Dynamics of Power.* Cambridge, MA: Schenkman Books, Inc., 1983.

Keating, Charles J. *Dealing with Difficult People.* Mahwah, NJ: Paulist Press, 1984.

Kottler, Jeffrey. *Beyond Blame.* San Francisco, CA: Jossey-Bass, 1994.

Linkemer, Bobbi. *Solving People Problems: The Essential Guide to Thinking and Working Smarter.* New York, NY: AMACOM, 2000.

Markman, Howard J., Stanley, Scott M., and Blumberg, Susan L. *Fighting for Your Marriage.* San Francisco, CA: Jossey-Bass, 2001.

McKinney, Bruce C., Kimsey, William D. and Fuller, Rex M. *Mediator Communication Competencies.* 4th Edition. Edina, MN: Burgess Publishing, 1995.

Muldoon, Brian. *The Heart of Conflict.* New York, NY: G. P. Putnam's Sons, 1996.

Nelson, Debra L. and Quick, James Campbell. *Organizational Behavior: Foundations, Realities, and Challenges.* St. Paul, MN: West Publishing Company, 1994.

Paulson, Terry L. *They Shoot Managers Don't They?* Berkeley, CA: Ten Speed Press, 1991.

Rubin, Jeffrey and Rubin, Carol. *When Families Fight.* New York, NY: William Morrow and Company, Inc, 1989.

Schmidt, Warren H. and Tannenbaum, Robert. "Managing Differences," *Harvard Business Review on Negotiation and Conflict Resolution.* Cambridge, MA: Harvard Business School Press, 2000.

Scott, Gini Graham. *Resolving Conflict with Others and Within Yourself.* Oakland, CA: New Harbinger Publications, Inc., 1990.

Tubbs, Stewart L. *A Systems Approach to Small Group Interaction*, 2nd Edition. New York, NY: Random House, 1984.

Viscott, David, M.D. *I Love You, Let's Work It Out.* New York, NY: Simon and Schuster, 1987.